Break Free

A Guide to Divorcing a Narcissist and Reclaiming Your Life

Emily R. Sterling

© **Copyright Emily R. Sterling 2023**

All rights reserved. The content contained within this book may not be reproduced, duplicated or transmitted without direct written permission from the author or the publisher.

ISBN: 978-0-6458852-6-2 (e-book)

ISBN: 979-8-8663450-3-8 (paperback)

Cover design by EM.

This publication is designed to provide accurate and authoritative information in regard to the subject matter covered. It is sold with the understanding that the author and the publisher are not engaged in rendering legal, accounting or other professional services. If legal advice or other expert assistance is required, the services of a competent professional person should be sought.

Contents

Introduction

Chapter 1: Understanding Narcissism

Defining narcissism: An overview of narcissistic personality disorder

Types of narcissism: Grandiose vs. vulnerable narcissism

Key characteristics and behaviors of narcissists

Debunking myths about narcissism

The impact of narcissism on relationships

Chapter 2: Recognizing Narcissistic Relationships

Early signs, red flags, and patterns in a narcissistic relationship

Emotional manipulation and gaslighting techniques

Some more on Grandiose (Overt) and Vulnerable (Covert) narcissism

The cycle of abuse and control

Chapter 3: Making the Decision to Leave

Assessing the situation: Evaluating the level of toxicity and abuse

Overcoming guilt and fear associated with leaving a narcissist

Creating a support system: Family, friends, and professional resources

Developing a safety plan and establishing boundaries

Gathering evidence and preparing for legal proceedings

What about the kids?

What to Do if Your Friends and Family Don't Understand

Chapter 4: Navigating the Legal Process

Securing legal representation experienced in dealing with narcissistic partners

Gathering evidence and presenting a strong case

Managing Court Proceedings and Potential Challenges

Coping with the financial aspects of divorce

Paying for a lawyer

Chapter 5: Co-parenting with a narcissist:

Protecting children from the conflict

Good Communication is Critical

Document everything

Protecting your children from the dispute

Chapter 6: Recovery and Healing

The importance of self-care during and after divorce

Dealing with trauma and rebuilding self-esteem

Therapeutic approaches for healing from narcissistic abuse

Understanding complex post-traumatic stress disorder

Embracing forgiveness and letting go of resentment

Chapter 7: Starting Over: Building a New Life

Rediscovering personal identity and values

Setting Goals and Envisioning a Brighter Future

Rebuilding social connections and fostering healthy relationships

Exploring new hobbies and interests

Embracing Personal Growth and Self-Empowerment

Conclusion

The Last Bit

About the Author

Introduction

In the intricate tapestry of Greek mythology, a timeless tale unfolds the profound complexities of self-absorption and the devastating consequences it can inflict upon the human soul. It is a story of Echo and Narcissus, a narrative that, in many ways, mirrors the harrowing journey of those who find themselves entangled in a marriage or relationship with a narcissistic partner.

Echo, a nymph renowned for her enchanting voice, was cursed to repeat the words of others, her voice reduced to mere echoes. Her longing for connection and her capacity for love was undeniable. Yet, her curse left her trapped in a world where her voice was but a reflection of others' words—a haunting reminder of her inability to be heard and understood.

And then there was Narcissus, a man of exquisite beauty who unknowingly embodied the very essence of his namesake. In his wanderings through the wilderness, he discovered his own reflection in a tranquil pool of water. Entranced by his own image, Narcissus became ensnared by an insatiable self-love, unable to tear himself away from the captivating reflection that held him captive.

As the story unfolds, we witness the tragic consequences of Narcissus's obsession with self and its profound impact on those who crossed his path. His rejection of the yearning and voiceless Echo and inability to connect with others beyond his own image ultimately led him to a lonely and tragic end.

The tale of Echo and Narcissus serves as an allegory—a stark warning that, even in the most enchanting of partnerships, the enchantment of a narcissist's self-absorption can leave their partner feeling like an echoing voice, unheard and unseen.

The toxic grip of narcissistic relationships is a suffocating embrace that leaves one feeling like Echo, their voice silenced and their needs echoing into the abyss. Much like the cursed nymph, those entangled with narcissistic partners often find themselves repeating the same pleas for understanding and empathy, only to be met with the self-absorbed reflection of a partner consumed by their own needs.

In the shadow of a narcissist's relentless self-love, the partner's true essence is eclipsed, much like Narcissus, who could see nothing beyond his own image. The relationship becomes one-sided, with the narcissist demanding constant admiration and attention, leaving their partner feeling invisible and insignificant.

But, as the ancient myth teaches us, the journey through the depths of such toxicity can lead to transformation. It is a journey that requires strength, resilience, and the reclamation of one's voice and self-worth. In the following pages, we will navigate the treacherous waters of divorcing a narcissist, striving to break free from the toxic grip, and find healing, empowerment, and a voice that resonates with authenticity.

The purpose of this book is to provide a guiding light through the labyrinth of divorcing a narcissistic partner, offering solace, understanding, and empowerment to those who have endured the tumultuous waters of such relationships. It is a beacon of hope for those who have felt trapped in the relentless storm of a narcissist's self-absorption, offering a path toward healing, happiness, and a brighter future.

In the following pages, the aim to empower individuals with knowledge, strategies, and insights to survive and thrive after divorcing a narcissistic partner. These relationships can leave deep scars, eroding self-esteem and causing emotional turmoil. The goal is to help you regain your sense of self, rebuild your life, and rediscover your innate strength and resilience.

Chapter One works through core concepts in ***understanding narcissism*** – key definitions and concepts to understand the characteristics and behaviors of those with narcissistic traits and narcissistic personality disorder.

Chapter Two examines ***recognizing narcissistic relationships***, the early signs and red flags that arise in relationships, and the impact of emotional manipulation and gaslighting.

Chapter Three looks at ***making the decision to leave*** and the support you will need.

In **Chapter Four**, ***navigating the legal process*** is the theme, working through securing legal representation, managing court proceedings, and coping with the financial aspects of divorce.

Chapter Five deals with the important task of ***co-parenting with a narcissist***, the importance of boundaries, communication, and focusing on the children's wellbeing.

Chapter Six works through ***healing and recovery***, the importance of self-care, dealing with trauma, and engaging in therapy.

Finally, **Chapter Seven** works through ***starting over and building a new life*** beyond your relationship with a narcissist.

Note that this book is written as an information guide only. It should not be read as advice specific to your personal circumstances. In fact, you will find no references to the law in this book. That is deliberate, where the law varies depending on where you live. You should consult a lawyer to obtain legal advice about your individual circumstances. Importantly, ***you should seek advice from a lawyer in your jurisdiction (area).***

This book also covers themes relating to recovery from relationships which cause trauma. It is important that you **don't attempt to self-diagnose** any feelings you may have and that you **seek therapeutic assistance from a qualified mental health professional** if you need assistance.

This book serves as a guide through the complexities of divorcing a narcissist, offering practical advice on legal, emotional, and psychological aspects. It sheds light on the dynamics of narcissistic abuse and provides tools to break free from the toxic grip, heal from past wounds, and ultimately find a path toward happiness and fulfillment.

As you turn the pages, may you find the wisdom and empowerment you seek to reclaim your voice, your worth, and your life. This book is a testament to the indomitable human spirit and the capacity for transformation, even in the face of the darkest challenges.

Chapter 1: Understanding Narcissism

Understanding narcissism is paramount in our quest for healthier relationships and emotional well-being. It gives us essential insights into a complex personality trait that can profoundly impact individuals and those around them. This process is not about passing judgment but equipping ourselves with the knowledge and tools to navigate relationships and life's challenges more effectively. It empowers us to build healthier connections, protect our emotional health, and contribute to the well-being of those around us.

Defining narcissism: An overview of narcissistic personality disorder

Narcissistic personality disorder (NPD) is a mental condition marked by a persistent tendency towards an inflated sense of self-importance, an overwhelming craving for admiration, and a reduced capacity to understand and share in the emotions of others.

People with Narcissistic personality disorder have an enlarged perception of their importance and a deep need for respect.

Now, many people have a conscious or subconscious need for admiration and adoration from others. This may not necessarily translate to narcissism (and frequently, it doesn't.). What sets a narcissist apart from other admiration loves is that this very factor about them dictates their behavior nearly everywhere they go. It determines how they present in social gatherings, talk, walk, conduct themselves, and treat others.

Irrespective of whether or not a narcissist can legitimately achieve the level of respect and admiration that they deem acceptable, they will attempt to take it from their environment, where the central conflict in their personality arises.

At its most basic level, you might take the following scenario.

Imagine wanting a box of chocolates so desperately but being unable to pay for it or obtain it in some other legitimate way. Imagine that despite being unable to pay for it, you are also unwilling to receive it in some other honest way, like genuinely befriending the chocolate vendor such that they may give you some (mostly because you think yourself far above and better than the chocolate vendor).

Still, you want it so badly that you will pretend to be the vendor's friend long enough for them to give you some chocolates. The plan works for a while, but masks slip because friendships can only be faked for so long.

So, the chocolate vendor finds out that you didn't like them, and they are only in your life for the chocolates, but you somehow convince them that it is their fault you don't want them enough. If they give you enough chocolates, you might like them enough. You back it up with some, make a show of vulnerability, and offer subtle praise that suggests that their chocolates are so delicious that you can't live without them.

So, the chocolate vendor forgives you several times, sometimes over several years, during which you hurt, abuse, talk down on, and generally mistreat them until they have had enough and finally summons the courage to unfriend you. So, you find another chocolate vendor and repeat the cycle.

But... Isn't this the same as high self-esteem?

It is easy for untrained eyes to mistake narcissism for high self-esteem. Because isn't the need of the ego a general one? Don't we all like to be loved and respected by our community? Don't we all strive to achieve a certain level of success and prominence as dictated by our society?

There are many people out there who are proud, maybe even arrogant. But this doesn't fundamentally mean they harm their loved ones. They may react very adversely to perceived and actual disrespect, but these things do not usually make a person a narcissist.

So, how do we define NPD?

The American Psychiatric Association's *Diagnostic and Statistical Manual of Mental Disorders, Fifth Edition* (*DSM-5*) defines NPD as comprising a pervasive pattern of grandiosity (in fantasy or behavior), a constant need for admiration, and a lack of empathy, beginning by early adulthood and present in a variety of contexts, as indicated by the presence of at least five of the following nine criteria:

- A grandiose sense of self-importance

- A preoccupation with fantasies of unlimited success, power, brilliance, beauty, or ideal love

- A belief that they are special and unique and can only be understood by, or should associate with, other special or high-status people or institutions

- A need for excessive admiration

- A sense of entitlement

- Interpersonally exploitive behavior

- A lack of empathy

- Envy of others or a belief that others are envious of them

- A demonstration of arrogant and haughty behaviors or attitudes

Types of narcissism: Grandiose vs. vulnerable narcissism

Over time, researchers have identified various subtypes of narcissism, with two prominent categories being **grandiose narcissism** and **vulnerable narcissism**. These categories are also sometimes described as overt or covert narcissism. Depending on your research, you will also see five types of narcissism. The research varies, and traits and diagnoses exist on a spectrum – that is, a range in severity from mild through to severe.

In this section, you will find information about these two distinct manifestations of narcissism – grandiose (overt) and vulnerable (covert) – with different characteristics, behaviors, and underlying psychological dynamics.

Grandiose narcissism is the more recognizable and stereotypical form of narcissism. Individuals with this subtype tend to exhibit an inflated sense of self-importance, a pervasive need for attention, and a belief in their own exceptional abilities. Some key characteristics and behaviors associated with grandiose narcissism are:

1. **Exaggerated Self-Importance:** Grandiose narcissists view themselves as superior to others in various aspects of life, whether in intelligence, attractiveness, or achievements. They often talk about their accomplishments and expect constant admiration and recognition.

2. **Manipulative Charm:** They can be charismatic and charming, especially when they want to win people over. Their charm can make it challenging for others to initially recognize their underlying narcissistic traits.

3. **Lack of Empathy:** Grandiose narcissists struggle to empathize with the emotions and needs of others. They may dismiss or belittle the concerns of those around them, focusing primarily on their own desires and feelings.

4. **Exploitative Behavior:** They may exploit others for personal gain, whether in relationships, friendships, or the workplace. They are often more interested in what they can get from others than in genuine connections.

5. **Fragile Self-Esteem:** Paradoxically, grandiose narcissists often have fragile self-esteem underneath their grandiose exterior. Criticism or rejection can deeply affect them, leading to defensive or aggressive reactions.

6. **Risk-Taking:** They tend to be more willing to take risks, believing they are immune to negative consequences. This can manifest in reckless behavior, especially when their ego is at stake.

Vulnerable narcissism, sometimes referred to as covert or fragile narcissism, represents a more subtle and complex form of narcissism. Individuals with this subtype are also preoccupied with their own importance but tend to exhibit traits associated with insecurity and hypersensitivity. Some key characteristics and behaviors associated with vulnerable narcissism are:

1. **Hypersensitivity to Criticism:** Vulnerable narcissists are highly sensitive to criticism, often interpreting it as a personal attack. They may become defensive or withdrawn in response to perceived slights.

2. **Self-Doubt:** Unlike grandiose narcissists who project unwavering confidence, those with vulnerable narcissism may struggle with self-doubt and feelings of inadequacy. They may secretly crave validation and approval.

3. **Social Withdrawal:** They may avoid social situations or relationships to protect themselves from potential rejection. Paradoxically, they desire social connection but are afraid of being hurt.

4. **Fantasies of Success:** Vulnerable narcissists may daydream about achieving greatness or recognition, which serves as a defense mechanism against their underlying self-doubt.

5. **Passive-Aggressiveness:** Instead of the overt aggression seen in grandiose narcissism, individuals with vulnerable narcissism may employ passive-aggressive tactics when they feel slighted or overlooked.

6. **Interpersonal Difficulties:** Their inability to handle criticism and their fragile self-esteem can strain relationships, leading to conflict and misunderstandings.

It's important to note that ***narcissism exists on a spectrum***, and individuals may exhibit a combination of grandiose and vulnerable narcissistic traits. Moreover, narcissism can be adaptive in moderation, as it can promote self-confidence and resilience. However, when narcissistic traits become extreme and interfere with a person's ability to form healthy relationships and function effectively in society, they may indicate narcissistic personality disorder.

Grandiose and vulnerable narcissism represent two distinct but interrelated facets of narcissistic personality traits. Understanding these subtypes can aid in recognizing and dealing with narcissistic behaviors in various contexts, from personal relationships to the workplace.

Key characteristics and behaviors of narcissists

Let us return briefly to those nine key characteristics and see what else we can learn.

A grandiose sense of self-importance is a defining characteristic of individuals with grandiose narcissism. It reflects an exaggerated belief in their own significance and abilities, often leading them to view themselves as unique and superior to others. These individuals constantly seek admiration and validation, expecting special treatment and privileges. This entitlement, coupled with a diminished capacity for empathy, can strain their relationships as they prioritize their own needs and desires over those of others.

Paradoxically, beneath this facade of self-assuredness lies a fragile self-esteem, making them highly sensitive to criticism and defensive in response to any perceived challenge to their self-image. Understanding and addressing this trait is vital for both individuals exhibiting it and those interacting with them, as it can significantly impact the quality of their relationships and overall well-being.

A prominent feature of narcissistic personality traits is a ***preoccupation with fantasies of unlimited success, power, brilliance, beauty, or ideal love***. Individuals exhibiting this trait often engage in elaborate daydreams or mental scenarios where they envision themselves achieving unparalleled levels of success, gaining absolute power, displaying exceptional brilliance, attaining unmatched physical beauty, or basking in a love that surpasses all others. These fantasies serve as a coping mechanism, allowing them to escape feelings of insecurity or inadequacy and bolster their fragile self-esteem.

People with these traits believe that by imagining these grandiose scenarios, they can momentarily fulfill their insatiable need for admiration and validation. However, this preoccupation with fantasies can have detrimental consequences, leading to unrealistic expectations and a detachment from reality. It may also hinder their ability to form genuine connections with others, as they may become more engrossed in their self-created worlds than in the real, imperfect people around them.

The belief that one is special and unique and, therefore, can only be truly understood by, or should exclusively associate with other special or high-status individuals or institutions is a characteristic trait associated with NPD. Individuals who hold this belief perceive themselves as exceptional and above the ordinary, leading them to seek out like-minded individuals or exclusive environments that they believe align with their elevated status.

This quest for association with the "elite" bolsters their fragile self-esteem and maintains the illusion of grandiosity. They may feel entitled to special treatment and admiration, leading to a sense of superiority over others. However, this belief often leads to social isolation and strained relationships, as their insistence on associating only with high-status individuals can alienate them from genuine, meaningful connections. It also perpetuates their narcissistic tendencies, reinforcing their grandiose self-image.

The ***incessant need for excessive admiration*** is a defining trait and plays a central role in the lives of individuals with NPD. Those with NPD have an insatiable thirst for admiration, continuously seeking validation, praise, and adoration from others to prop up their fragile self-esteem. This relentless desire for attention can manifest in various ways, such as a constant need for compliments, unwavering attention-seeking behavior, and a preoccupation with being recognized and admired.

This need for excessive admiration often drives individuals with NPD to engage in manipulative tactics and attention-seeking behaviors. They may go to great lengths to ensure they are the center of attention in social settings, often monopolizing conversations and belittling or dismissing others to assert their dominance. They may also cultivate an image of success and superiority to elicit admiration, even if it means exaggerating their accomplishments or creating a facade of grandiosity.

However, this pursuit of admiration comes at a significant cost. It can lead to shallow and transactional relationships, as individuals with NPD tend to view others primarily as sources of validation rather than as individuals with their own needs and feelings. It can also result in chronic feelings of emptiness, as no amount of admiration can ever truly fill the void caused by their fragile self-esteem.

A ***pervasive sense of entitlement*** can also be found in individuals with narcissistic traits. Those with NPD believe they inherently deserve special treatment, admiration, and privileges simply by virtue of their existence. This entitlement extends to all aspects of their lives, from personal relationships to professional endeavors.

Individuals with NPD often expect preferential treatment from others and may become frustrated or angry when their expectations are unmet. They believe that the rules that apply to everyone else do not apply to them, leading to a disregard for societal norms and an inflated sense of their own importance. This sense of entitlement can manifest as an insistence on being the center of attention, a belief that they deserve success without putting in the necessary effort, or a lack of consideration for the needs and feelings of others.

While entitlement is a central feature of NPD, it can also create significant challenges in interpersonal relationships. Friends, family members, and colleagues may struggle to relate to or collaborate with individuals who constantly demand special treatment and validation. This entitlement can strain relationships, contributing to frustration and resentment in those who interact with individuals with NPD.

Interpersonally exploitative behavior is a significant trait. Individuals with NPD often engage in manipulative and self-serving actions in their interactions with others, seeking to exploit relationships for their own benefit. This behavior can take various forms, such as using others for personal gain, disregarding the needs and feelings of others, and taking advantage of people's vulnerabilities.

One common manifestation of interpersonally exploitive behavior in individuals with NPD is the relentless pursuit of admiration and attention. They may establish relationships with people solely to boost their self-esteem and ego, often discarding individuals when they no longer serve this purpose. These individuals may also exploit others for material or social advantages, viewing people as tools to achieve their goals rather than as individuals with their own aspirations and emotions.

Furthermore, individuals with NPD often lack genuine empathy and may manipulate others to meet their own needs. They may use charm, flattery, or even emotional manipulation to achieve their objectives, often leaving a trail of hurt feelings and damaged relationships in their wake.

A striking and defining characteristic of NPD is ***a profound and persistent lack of empathy***. Individuals with NPD have difficulty understanding and connecting with the emotions, needs, and experiences of others. Their emotional landscape is primarily centered around their own desires, aspirations, and self-worth, leaving little room for genuine empathy toward those around them.

This lack of empathy can manifest in various ways. Individuals with NPD may dismiss or belittle the feelings and concerns of others, viewing them as inconsequential compared to their own. They may struggle to take the perspective of others, making it challenging to comprehend why someone might be hurt or upset by their actions or words. This lack of emotional attunement can lead to insensitive and callous behavior, often causing pain and frustration in their relationships.

Moreover, individuals with NPD may manipulate others to serve their own needs, exploiting their emotions without genuine concern for the consequences. They can appear charming and empathetic when it suits their purposes, but these displays of empathy are often superficial and calculated rather than authentic expressions of understanding and compassion.

A complex and noteworthy aspect of NPD is ***the envy of others or a pervasive belief that others harbor envy toward oneself***. Individuals with NPD often struggle with profound feelings of inadequacy and a fragile sense of self-esteem beneath their grandiose facade. This insecurity can manifest as envy towards those who appear to possess the qualities or achievements they desire. They may resent others' success, attractiveness, or happiness, viewing it as a threat to their own self-worth.

Simultaneously, individuals with NPD frequently project their own feelings of envy onto others. They assume that people around them envy their perceived superiority, even when no evidence supports this belief. This conviction of being envied reinforces their inflated self-image and helps shield them from confronting their deep-seated insecurities.

This dual dynamic of experiencing envy while believing others envy them can create a toxic interpersonal environment. It fosters mistrust and may lead to unhealthy competition or manipulation in relationships, as individuals with NPD may go to great lengths to prove their superiority or protect themselves from imagined threats.

Demonstrating arrogant and haughty behaviors or attitudes is a notable trait within the spectrum of NPD. Individuals with NPD often exhibit an inflated sense of self-importance and entitlement, which can lead to the overt display of arrogance and haughtiness in their interactions with others.

Arrogant behavior in those with NPD may manifest as a consistent belief in their own superiority and a tendency to belittle or dismiss the thoughts, opinions, or achievements of others. They may seek out opportunities to showcase their supposed brilliance or accomplishments, often dominating conversations and conversations with a condescending tone.

Haughtiness, on the other hand, reflects an attitude of disdain or contempt towards those they perceive as beneath them. Individuals with NPD may exhibit a patronizing demeanor, viewing themselves as an elite group and looking down upon others as inferior. This attitude can contribute to strained relationships, as it creates a power dynamic that is neither respectful nor empathetic.

Debunking myths about narcissism

It is essential to consider some myths about narcissism to foster a better understanding of this complex personality trait and its associated disorders. Here are seven key points to clarify common misconceptions:

1. **Narcissism is not just about vanity:** While narcissism does involve a heightened sense of self-importance and a desire for admiration, it goes beyond mere vanity. It encompasses a range of behaviors and attitudes, including a lack of empathy, a sense of entitlement, and a tendency to exploit others for personal gain. Narcissism is a multifaceted personality trait with deep-seated psychological roots, and it can manifest in various ways beyond superficial self-admiration.

2. **Not all narcissists are the same:** There is a spectrum of narcissistic traits, and individuals with narcissism may vary significantly in their behavior and impact on others. Some may exhibit more overt, grandiose narcissism, characterized by arrogance and an overt need for attention. In contrast, others may display covert or vulnerable narcissism, marked by insecurity, self-doubt, and a fragile self-esteem. Understanding these variations is crucial for accurately assessing and addressing narcissistic traits in individuals.

3. **Narcissism exists on a spectrum:** It's important to recognize that narcissism is not an all-or-nothing trait. Many people possess some narcissistic traits to varying degrees, which can be adaptive in moderation. It becomes problematic when these traits are extreme and pervasive, leading to difficulties in

functioning and maintaining healthy relationships. Thus, the presence of narcissistic traits does not necessarily mean someone has NPD, and a diagnosis should be made by qualified mental health professionals based on a comprehensive assessment.

4. **Narcissism is not always a choice:** While narcissistic behaviors can be harmful and frustrating to others, it's important to recognize that individuals with narcissistic traits or NPD may not consciously choose to behave that way. These traits often have roots in early life experiences, and individuals may have developed maladaptive coping mechanisms as a result. Understanding that narcissism can be deeply ingrained and, in some cases, linked to past trauma or upbringing can lead to a more empathetic approach when dealing with individuals exhibiting these traits.

5. **Narcissism is not limited to a specific gender:** Narcissistic traits can be found in individuals of any gender. While some stereotypes may portray narcissism as more prevalent in one gender over another, it is not inherently tied to gender. Both men and women can exhibit narcissistic behaviors, and the traits manifest similarly regardless of gender.

6. **Narcissism does not guarantee success:** While some narcissists may succeed in certain areas due to their confidence and ambition, narcissism does not guarantee success in all aspects of life. In fact, the arrogance and lack of empathy associated with narcissism can hinder collaboration and damage relationships, potentially leading to professional and personal

setbacks. Many factors influence success, and narcissism is just one component of a complex personality.

7. **Narcissism is not always easily recognizable:** While some individuals with narcissistic traits may display overt and noticeable behaviors, others can be adept at concealing their narcissistic tendencies. Covert or vulnerable narcissists, for example, may appear modest or self-effacing on the surface while harboring feelings of superiority and entitlement beneath. Recognizing narcissism may require a deeper understanding of underlying behaviors and attitudes rather than relying solely on outward appearances, emphasizing the importance of careful observation and assessment when identifying narcissistic traits in individuals.

Debunking myths about narcissism is essential for several reasons. Myths and misconceptions often perpetuate stigma and stereotypes, hindering empathy and support for individuals genuinely struggling with narcissistic traits or NPD. Recognizing that narcissism exists on a spectrum and can manifest in various ways allows for a more nuanced perspective. Moreover, accurate information about narcissism empowers mental health professionals, educators, and the general public to address the issue more effectively.

The impact of narcissism on relationships

While it's important to note that narcissism exists on a spectrum, and not all individuals with narcissistic traits or tendencies will exhibit the same behaviors to the same degree, narcissism can have a profound and often detrimental impact on personal and professional relationships. In some cases, narcissistic traits can be adaptive in moderation, but when they become extreme and pervasive the impact on those around them can be seriously problematic.

Here are some of the key ways in which narcissism can affect relationships.

Difficulty with empathy is a key factor that impacts relationships and interpersonal interactions. Individuals with NPD often find it challenging to empathize with the emotions, needs, and experiences of others, primarily because they are preoccupied with their own desires and self-importance.

This lack of empathy means that narcissists may struggle to truly understand or share the feelings of those around them. They may dismiss or belittle the concerns and perspectives of others, prioritizing their own needs and feelings. This self-centeredness can lead to a profound sense of invalidation and neglect in their relationships.

Furthermore, the difficulty with empathy often results in behaviors that are hurtful to others, as narcissists may exploit or manipulate individuals for personal gain without regard for the emotional impact. This exploitation can range from emotional manipulation to more overt forms of manipulation and deceit.

In essence, the limited capacity for empathy in individuals with NPD can make it challenging for them to form healthy, meaningful, and mutually satisfying relationships.

Manipulation and exploitation are prevalent behaviors, and individuals with NPD often employ these tactics to fulfill their unrelenting need for admiration, power, and control.

Manipulation can take many forms, ranging from subtle emotional manipulation to more overt and calculated strategies. Narcissists may use charm, flattery, or deceit to gain an advantage or manipulate others into meeting their desires. Their manipulative behaviors often serve to maintain their self-image as superior and all-important.

Exploitation involves taking advantage of people for personal gain, often without consideration for the consequences or well-being of others. Narcissists view individuals as tools to fulfill their own needs and may exploit their vulnerabilities, resources, or emotions to achieve their goals. This exploitation can occur in various contexts, from personal relationships to the workplace.

In relationships, manipulation and exploitation erode trust and create an unhealthy dynamic characterized by power imbalances. These behaviors can lead to emotional, psychological, and sometimes even financial harm to the individuals involved.

An ***inflated sense of entitlement*** is a prominent feature and one of the core characteristics that can deeply affect relationships and interactions with individuals who have this condition. Those with NPD often harbor an unwavering belief that they inherently deserve special treatment, admiration, and privileges that exceed those granted to others. This entitlement extends to all aspects of their lives, from personal relationships to professional endeavors.

Individuals with an inflated sense of entitlement may expect preferential treatment from others, believing that rules, norms, and societal standards don't apply to them. This can result in a disregard for the feelings, rights, and boundaries of others, as their own desires and needs take precedence. This entitled attitude can foster resentment and frustration in their relationships, creating an unequal power dynamic and leading to a lack of reciprocity.

Due to this condition's distinctive traits and behaviors, ***interpersonal conflict*** often accompanies NPD. Individuals with NPD frequently exhibit arrogance, a lack of empathy, and a sense of entitlement, all of which can contribute to conflicts in their relationships.

Their arrogance and haughty attitudes may lead to condescending and dismissive behavior, causing frustration and resentment in their interactions with others. They may prioritize their own desires and needs above those of their partners, leading to power struggles and disputes.

Furthermore, their inability to empathize with others' emotions and perspectives can make communication challenging. They may struggle to understand why their actions or words hurt or upset others, resulting in repeated conflicts that remain unresolved.

The sense of entitlement often leads to demands for special treatment or unwavering admiration, causing friction as they disregard the feelings and boundaries of those around them. Partners and loved ones may feel emotionally drained and unappreciated, leading to ongoing conflicts and emotional distress.

Shallow and superficial connections are a common outcome of interactions. Narcissists often struggle to form deep and meaningful relationships due to their self-centeredness and lack of genuine empathy.

In these shallow connections, narcissists may interact primarily for personal gain, validation, or admiration. They may superficially charm others to achieve their goals, creating the illusion of a deep connection without the substance to support it. These interactions can leave others feeling used and emotionally unfulfilled.

Furthermore, narcissists may view people as tools for their own validation rather than individuals with their own needs and feelings. As a result, their relationships tend to lack depth, emotional intimacy, and reciprocity. They may prioritize their own desires and rarely invest in the emotional well-being of others, leading to one-sided and transactional connections.

The absence of genuine emotional connection and intimacy can lead to loneliness and dissatisfaction for those interacting with narcissists. It also reinforces the perception that narcissists prioritize their own needs above all else, perpetuating a cycle of shallow and unfulfilling relationships.

Fragile self-esteem is a paradoxical aspect that often remains hidden beneath the grandiose exterior. Individuals with NPD may exhibit an exaggerated sense of self-importance, seeking constant admiration and validation from others. However, beneath this facade lies a profound insecurity and vulnerability, which characterizes their fragile self-esteem.

This fragility is rooted in deep-seated feelings of inadequacy and a fear of being exposed as less than perfect. Criticism or any challenge to their self-image can provoke intense defensive reactions, including anger, deflection, or withdrawal. The need for external validation becomes a relentless pursuit to shield themselves from confronting their inner feelings of unworthiness.

Ironically, this fragile self-esteem drives many narcissistic behaviors observed in individuals with NPD. They become preoccupied with proving their superiority and avoiding situations that might trigger feelings of inadequacy. Paradoxically, their relentless quest for admiration can undermine their relationships and personal growth, as it often involves manipulating and exploiting others.

Relationship instability is a common outcome when one or both partners exhibit narcissistic traits or suffer from NPD. Narcissistic individuals often struggle to maintain healthy and enduring connections due to their self-centered behaviors and emotional dynamics.

The narcissist's relentless need for admiration and attention is one key factor contributing to relationship instability. Their constant craving for validation can lead to a pattern of seeking out new sources of admiration, which can result in infidelity or abrupt relationship changes.

Furthermore, the narcissist's inability to empathize with their partner's emotions and needs can create ongoing conflicts and misunderstandings. Their lack of emotional reciprocity and self-centered focus can make their partner feel undervalued and emotionally neglected.

Additionally, narcissists may exhibit a sense of entitlement and an expectation that their needs should always be prioritized. This can lead to power struggles and one-sided dynamics within the relationship, further destabilizing it.

Relationship instability with narcissistic individuals often follows a cyclical pattern of intense charm, followed by disillusionment, conflict, and, in some cases, abrupt endings. It can leave partners feeling emotionally drained and unfulfilled, ultimately leading to the deterioration of the relationship.

With so many apparent negative traits, why do people fall in love with those with narcissistic traits or NPD? At face value, they don't seem like very nice people, and yet, every day, divorce lawyers all over the world are assisting people to extract themselves from these relationships. So, let's look at what it's like to fall in love with a narcissist and to understand how to look out for the red flags you're your relationship may not be healthy.

Chapter 2: Recognizing Narcissistic Relationships

People may fall in love with narcissists for various reasons, even though such relationships can be challenging and often tumultuous. It may be that you do not know what you have gotten yourself into until it's too late.

Narcissists often possess an ***initial charm, charisma, and confidence*** that can be very appealing. They may be skilled at creating a captivating first impression, drawing others in with their self-assuredness and charisma.

In the early stages of a relationship, narcissists often engage in what's known as the ***"idealization" phase***. During this time, they shower their partner with attention, affection, and compliments, making the other person feel special and loved.

People who have been through emotionally challenging experiences, such as a breakup or personal loss, may be particularly vulnerable to the charms of a narcissist. The narcissist's attention and flattery can provide a ***temporary emotional escape or validation during a difficult time***.

Narcissists often exude a ***high level of self-confidence***, which can be attractive to individuals who may struggle with their own self-esteem. Some people are drawn to this confidence and may see it as a source of inspiration or support.

Narcissists can be ***skilled manipulators*** who use tactics like gaslighting or intermittent reinforcement to keep their partners invested in the relationship. This behavior can create confusion and make it difficult for their partners to leave.

Some individuals enter relationships with narcissists, **believing that they can change or "fix" the narcissistic behaviors**. They may see the narcissist's potential or hold onto the early idealization phase, hoping it will return.

The **unpredictability** of narcissistic relationships, characterized by highs and lows, can be emotionally intense and addictive. This can make it challenging for individuals to break free from the cycle.

It's important to note that while people may initially fall in love with narcissists for various reasons, these relationships often become emotionally taxing and even harmful over time. Recognizing the patterns of narcissistic behavior and their impact is crucial.

Early signs, red flags, and patterns in a narcissistic relationship

If it seems too good to be true, it probably is.

Let's meet **Kate and Simon** and see how their relationship evolves.

An enthusiastic and charismatic man, Simon recently met Kate at a social gathering. Their connection was instant, and sparks flew between them. However, as their budding romance progressed, Kate noticed something peculiar - Simon's excessive affection.

Simon seemed utterly smitten with Kate, showering her with compliments, gifts, and affectionate gestures at an alarming rate.

While Kate initially appreciated the attention, she couldn't help but feel that things were moving too quickly. Simon's constant affection began to invade her personal space, leaving her feeling overwhelmed and uneasy.

For instance, after only a few dates, Simon surprised Kate with a bouquet of her favorite flowers delivered to her workplace, followed by a heartfelt love letter. While these gestures were sweet, Kate felt her boundaries were being pushed. She realized what initially seemed like a whirlwind romance made her uncomfortable. But at the same time, Kate was caught up in the romance, willing to ignore those feelings and enjoy being showered with affection.

As Simon and Kate's relationship continued to evolve, Kate began to notice a series of perplexing occurrences - the little things that didn't quite add up. At first, these incidents seemed minor and insignificant, but Kate couldn't shake the feeling that something was amiss. It soon became evident that these peculiar events were not accidents; they were deliberate actions meant to upset her.

For instance, Kate would find her cherished coffee mug mysteriously chipped, her favorite song playing at an unusually high volume when she entered the room, or her phone missing, only to reappear in an unexpected place. These seemingly small and random actions left Kate confused and frustrated, especially given the stark contrast to the initial stages of their relationship, characterized by overwhelming affection and warmth.

Kate had always been known for her outspoken and confident nature, a trait that initially drew Simon to her. In their relationship's early stages, he admired her assertiveness and praised her for being unapologetically herself. Their connection had been built on a foundation of mutual respect and admiration.

However, as time passed, Kate began to notice a change in how she was treated. Her once-admired, outspoken nature was now met with criticism and even ridicule. Simon had started to belittle her opinions, mock her for being too vocal, and dismiss her thoughts as insignificant. It felt as though something had shifted, leaving Kate bewildered and hurt.

In the early days of their relationship, Kate and Simon had shared a sense of togetherness and mutual support. They prioritized each other's feelings and tried to create a harmonious household. However, over time, Kate noticed a significant shift in their priorities.

Their once-shared experiences now seemed to take a backseat. Simon's attention was increasingly focused elsewhere, and he appeared less interested in Kate's daily life and emotions. When Kate had a stressful day and sought solace in quietness, Simon interpreted it as the "silent treatment," even when she explicitly explained that she was overwhelmed by stress and not trying to withdraw from him.

Kate felt that her feelings were no longer a priority in the household. Simon's apparent disregard for her emotional well-being left her feeling isolated and misunderstood. The shift in their dynamic had eroded the sense of shared experiences they had once cherished.

At the same time, Simon had started to insert himself into every aspect of Kate's life. He wanted to be involved in her daily routines, social circles, and hobbies. While Kate valued their closeness, she began to feel that her boundaries were constantly being breached. It was as if

Simon was fighting for a spot in her life that he didn't reciprocate on his own.

The imbalance left Kate feeling overwhelmed and her own boundaries neglected. She recognized that she couldn't even approach Simon's boundaries, let alone breach them. It was as though their relationship had become one-sided, with Kate struggling to maintain her independence and personal space.

Kate had also noticed that Simon occasionally did selfish or even outright wrong and unpleasant things, leaving her bewildered and hurt. When Kate confronted him about these actions, expecting acknowledgment or an apology, Simon often denied the obvious or downplayed the situation.

For instance, there was an occasion when Simon had made plans with Kate but canceled at the last minute without a valid reason. When Kate expressed her disappointment, Simon attempted to laugh it off, dismissing her feelings as if they were unimportant. If Kate persisted in seeking an explanation or acknowledgment, Simon would subtly shift the blame, making Kate feel she was overreacting or being unreasonable.

This pattern left Kate feeling frustrated and unheard. She found herself caught in a situation where addressing Simon's wrongdoings could lead to her being labeled as the "bad guy" in that instance, making her hesitant to speak up about her feelings and concerns.

As their relationship progressed, Kate couldn't help but notice a striking change in Simon's behavior. Simon, who had once been modest and reserved, had transformed into someone who walked around like a peacock, displaying exhibitionist tendencies and attitudes. He seemed to constantly seek attention and admiration in private and on social media.

Simon's social media presence had become a reflection of his exhibitionist tendencies. He would excessively post about himself, showcasing his life in a carefully curated and somewhat artificial manner. Kate felt he was trying to build a persona that didn't align with the Simon she knew. It was as if he were insistent on presenting a particular image of their relationship to the world, which felt fake and exaggerated.

The pressure to conform to Simon's crafted image left Kate feeling suffocated and inauthentic. She sensed that their relationship was becoming a performance for others rather than an authentic connection between two individuals.

Notably, Kate had often observed a stark contrast in Simon's behavior when interacting with others compared to how he treated her. Simon seemed to possess an innate ability to consistently present himself as the perfect and likable individual when in the company of others. He knew how to impress people, leaving them with the impression that he was charming and gracious.

However, Kate couldn't help but feel that this charming demeanor was rarely directed at her. Behind closed doors, Simon's behavior was often far from pleasant. He could be critical, dismissive, and even hurtful at times, creating a stark contrast to the confident and graceful persona he displayed to others.

Kate felt trapped in a situation where Simon's true nature was hidden from the outside world. Given the charming image he projected, she knew that if she were to confide in others about his behavior, they might find it hard to believe.

There are several red flags in this relationship – the excessive affection to start, the odd little things that start to occur, the stark contrast in how the relationship commenced, a shift in who is the priority in the household, the way Simon inserts himself into every part of Kates world; selfish, wrong or hurtful things that occur; the presentation to others as perfect and the need to exhibit the ideal existence.

While a person might not experience all these behaviors, they are important red flags to look for. Having said that – it's easy to describe behaviors from an objective point of view. Once you are in the relationship, though, it is hard to see, and over time, you become conditioned to a new form of normal.

Emotional manipulation and gaslighting techniques

Emotional manipulation and ***gaslighting*** are terms you often hear when discussing relationships with individuals with narcissistic traits or NPD. These are tactics often employed to control and manipulate others. These behaviors can profoundly damage the mental and emotional well-being of those on the receiving end.

Let's have a look at these two concepts in more detail.

Emotional manipulation is a complex and harmful tactic. One of the key components of emotional manipulation is "***love-bombing***."

In the early stages of a relationship, narcissists employ love-bombing to create an intense emotional connection with their target. They shower the person with extravagant displays of affection, compliments, and lavish gifts. This inundation of love and attention is designed to foster a profound sense of emotional dependency, making the target feel adored and special. However, it's crucial to understand that love-bombing is not a genuine display of affection but a calculated strategy to gain control.

The manipulator often transitions into the "***devaluation***" phase as the relationship progresses. During this stage, they employ tactics like criticism, humiliation, and the withdrawal of affection to systematically erode the target's self-esteem. This devaluation creates an emotional dependency on the manipulator, as the target becomes increasingly desperate for the return of the love and validation they received during the love-bombing phase.

Guilt-tripping is another manipulation technique frequently used by narcissists. They exploit the target's empathy and sense of obligation by playing the victim or referencing past favors. This behavior creates guilt-induced compliance, where the target feels obligated to meet the manipulator's demands, further solidifying the manipulator's control.

The ***silent treatment*** is yet another tactic used to maintain dominance. By ignoring or withholding communication, the narcissist exerts control and punishes the target for perceived wrongdoings or deviations from their desires.

Gaslighting, a particularly insidious form of manipulation, involves denying or distorting reality to make the target doubt their own perceptions and experiences. It leaves the target feeling confused, disoriented, and increasingly dependent on the manipulator's version of reality.

One of the core elements of gaslighting is "***denial and distortion***." Gaslighters adamantly deny the reality of events or conversations, even when there is clear evidence to the contrary. They may manipulate facts and details to align with their narrative, leaving the target disoriented and doubting their recollection.

Another common gaslighting technique is "***blame-shifting***." Gaslighters deflect responsibility by blaming the target, causing them to question their actions or emotions. Statements like "You're too sensitive" or "You're overreacting" invalidate the target's feelings and perceptions, further eroding their self-trust.

Gaslighters also employ "***minimization***" to belittle the significance of the target's emotions or experiences. By downplaying these feelings, they make the target feel their concerns are inconsequential, leaving them isolated and unsure of their own emotional responses.

Withholding information is another gaslighting tactic used to maintain control. By keeping the target in the dark about certain facts or events, gaslighters create confusion and doubt in the target's mind. This control over information reinforces their dominance.

"***Projection***" is a particularly insidious form of gaslighting where the manipulator projects their negative qualities or behaviors onto the target. This projection makes the target feel responsible for the gaslighter's actions or emotions, further destabilizing their sense of self.

Gaslighters often resort to "***isolation***" by separating the target from friends and family. This isolation makes the target more vulnerable and reliant on the gaslighter's version of reality, as they lack external perspectives to validate their own experiences.

In the case of Kate and Simon, emotional manipulation and gaslighting could explain why Kate may struggle to recognize Simon's behaviors as harmful.

Throughout their relationship, Simon had perfected the art of emotional manipulation. He knew just when to employ love-bombing tactics, showering Kate with affection and compliments during their early days together. This left Kate feeling cherished and special, creating a strong emotional bond. However, as time passed, Simon began to devalue Kate. He would make subtle, hurtful comments about her appearance or decisions, always disguised as jokes or playful banter. When Kate expressed hurt or confusion, Simon would employ gaslighting techniques. He'd deny ever making such comments or insist that Kate was being too sensitive. This left Kate doubting her own perception of reality, making her believe that maybe she was indeed overreacting.

Simon was also skilled at blame-shifting. Whenever a disagreement arose, he would turn the tables on Kate, making her feel guilty for raising concerns or expressing her feelings. He'd say things like, "You always bring up problems" or "You're ruining our relationship with your insecurities." These comments left Kate feeling responsible for their conflicts and made her hesitant to bring up any issues, as she feared being labeled as the problem.

Additionally, Simon isolated Kate from her friends and family by subtly criticizing them or creating conflicts within those relationships. He made her believe he was the only one who truly cared for her, reinforcing her emotional dependency on him. When Kate tried to discuss her concerns, Simon would engage in denial and distortion. He'd insist that he was the perfect partner and that any issues in their relationship were entirely her fault. This consistent manipulation left Kate feeling trapped, unable to see the harmful nature of Simon's behaviors because he had systematically eroded her self-esteem, self-trust, and ability to discern reality.

In this way, emotional manipulation and gaslighting created a toxic cycle where Kate struggled to perceive Simon's behaviors as bad despite their detrimental impact on her emotional well-being.

Some more on Grandiose (Overt) and Vulnerable (Covert) narcissism

Having delved into the life of Kate and Simon, let's pause here and come back to our two sub-types of NPD – grandiose (overt) and vulnerable (covert) narcissism and consider those in the context of Kate and Simon's relationship. As we saw in Chapter One, while both subtypes share core narcissistic traits, they manifest in different ways.

A conspicuous display of narcissistic traits characterizes ***overt narcissism***. Individuals with overt narcissistic tendencies exhibit grandiosity, arrogance, and an overwhelming sense of entitlement. They firmly believe they are exceptional and superior to others, often seeking admiration and attention at every opportunity.

In social interactions, they are notably attention-seeking, using flamboyant behaviors, boastfulness, and self-promotion to garner admiration and validation. Overt narcissists tend to dominate conversations, steering them towards topics highlighting their achievements, leaving little room for others to contribute or feel valued. This self-centeredness extends to their diminished ability to empathize with others, a common trait among all narcissists. They struggle to understand or genuinely care about the feelings and needs of those around them, often prioritizing their own desires.

These self-centered and dominant behaviors frequently strain relationships, as overt narcissists tend to exploit others for personal gain and can be manipulative, making it challenging to maintain healthy and mutually satisfying connections.

Covert narcissism is characterized by a more subtle and concealed expression of narcissistic traits. Individuals with covert narcissistic tendencies often present themselves as reserved, modest, and even shy. However, beneath this seemingly unassuming exterior lies a deep sense of entitlement and self-absorption. Unlike their overt counterparts, covert narcissists employ a different set of tactics. They may adopt a victim mentality, portraying themselves as misunderstood or mistreated by others.

This manipulation can elicit sympathy from those around them, ultimately serving their needs while deflecting responsibility for their actions. Covert narcissists also use passive-aggressive techniques to achieve their goals, avoiding direct confrontation while expecting others to satisfy their desires. They may appear self-sacrificing on the surface but maintain underlying expectations of others meeting their needs. Additionally, covert narcissists excel at emotional manipulation, skillfully playing on the emotions of those in their orbit to maintain a sense of power and control.

This hidden manipulation can make it challenging for individuals to recognize these behaviors and protect their emotional well-being.

Both overt and covert narcissists can be challenging to have relationships with, as their self-centeredness and lack of empathy can lead to emotional and psychological harm for those close to them. Understanding these subtypes can help individuals identify narcissistic behaviors in others, take steps to protect their well-being, and establish healthier boundaries.

Let's return to Simon and Kate and look at some examples of Simon's overt and covert behaviors.

Overt Narcissistic Behaviors:

1. **Grandiosity and Attention-Seeking:** Simon often dominated conversations and gatherings with his constant need for attention. He frequently boasted about his achievements and talents, making it clear that he believed himself to be exceptional. During social events, he would steer discussions toward topics that showcased his accomplishments, leaving little room for others to contribute or feel valued.

2. **Lack of Empathy and Exploitative Behavior:** Despite Kate's clearly expressed feelings and needs, Simon consistently demonstrated a lack of empathy. He frequently dismissed her emotions and concerns, seemingly indifferent to her well-being. In addition, he would exploit Kate's desire to please him by

making unreasonable demands and expecting her to cater to his every whim, often without reciprocating in kind.

3. **Arrogance and Entitlement:** Simon displayed a noticeable sense of entitlement and arrogance in his interactions with Kate. He believed he deserved special treatment and often expected Kate to cater to his every need and desire. He rarely acknowledged her contributions or made an effort to reciprocate, reinforcing his belief in his superiority.

Covert Narcissistic Behaviors:

1. **Hidden Insecurities and Victim Mentality:** Simon concealed a deep sense of entitlement and self-absorption behind his reserved and modest exterior. He would adopt a victim mentality when confronted about his behavior, portraying himself as misunderstood or mistreated. He subtly manipulated Kate's sympathy, making her feel guilty for raising concerns or expressing her feelings.

2. **Passive-Aggression and Emotional Manipulation:** Rather than openly seeking attention, Simon used passive-aggressive tactics to gain control and admiration. He often appeared self-sacrificing on the surface, but beneath this facade, he expected others to cater to his desires without expressing them directly. Simon was adept at emotional manipulation, playing on Kate's emotions to maintain a sense of power and control in the relationship.

3. **Gaslighting and Manipulative Silence:** Simon would use gaslighting tactics, such as denying or distorting past conversations or events. For instance, when Kate tried to

address issues in their relationship, he often claimed that they never had such conversations or that she was misremembering. Additionally, Simon employed manipulative silence as a means of control. When confronted with Kate's concerns, he would often give her the silent treatment, leaving her feeling isolated and doubting her own perceptions and emotions.

The cycle of abuse and control

We'll round out this chapter with information about the cycle of abuse and control and why it can be tricky to recognize the behavior and, more importantly, challenging to end the relationship.

The cycle of abuse and control is a ***pattern of behavior commonly observed in abusive relationships***. It typically consists of four main phases:

1. **Tension-Building Phase:** In this initial phase, tension begins to mount in the relationship. Minor conflicts, misunderstandings, or stressors may trigger the abuser's frustration or anger. During this stage, the victim often senses the tension and may try to avoid further conflict by walking on eggshells or complying with the abuser's demands. Communication becomes strained, and the victim may feel a growing sense of fear and unease.

2. **Explosive Incident Phase:** The tension escalates to a breaking point, leading to an explosive incident of abuse. This incident can take various forms, including physical violence,

verbal abuse, emotional manipulation, or sexual assault. The abuser's anger and aggression are unleashed, causing significant harm to the victim. This phase is marked by the actual abuse and its immediate aftermath.

3. **Honeymoon or Reconciliation Phase:** Following the abusive incident, the abuser often expresses remorse and seeks reconciliation. They may apologize, promise to change, or shower the victim with affection and gifts. During this phase, the victim may be hopeful that the abuse will stop, and they may believe the abuser's apologies and promises. This creates a temporary sense of relief and normalcy in the relationship.

4. **Calm or Tension-Reduction Phase:** The relationship temporarily returns to a calmer state in this final phase. The tension decreases, and the couple may experience a period of relative peace and harmony. However, this calm is short-lived, as the cycle begins anew with the tension-building phase. Over time, the cycle often repeats, with the abuse becoming more frequent and severe.

It's important to note that the ***cycle of abuse and control can vary in duration and intensity***, and not all abusive relationships follow this exact pattern.

Recognizing abusive behavior and finding the strength to end an abusive relationship can be a profoundly challenging and complex journey for many individuals. ***Several factors contribute to the difficulty of both recognizing and leaving such relationships.***

Firstly, abusers are adept at ***manipulation and control***. They employ various tactics, including gaslighting, where they distort reality and make the victim doubt their own perceptions. This manipulation creates confusion, making it challenging for victims to recognize the abuse they are experiencing. Abusers may downplay their actions, blaming external factors or claiming the victim is overly sensitive or mistaken.

Another complicating factor is the ***gradual escalation of abuse***. Abusive behavior often starts subtly and progressively intensifies over time. Initially, it may manifest as occasional emotional or verbal insults, which victims might dismiss as isolated incidents or attribute to stress or temporary relationship issues. As the abuse becomes more frequent and severe, victims may struggle to reconcile the abusive behavior with the person they initially fell in love with, further delaying recognition.

Emotional investment plays a significant role in the difficulty of recognizing and leaving abusive relationships. Victims may genuinely love their abusers and have shared experiences and memories that make it challenging to accept the reality of the abuse. This emotional attachment can lead to denial, as victims may cling to the hope that their abuser will change, and that the relationship can be salvaged.

Abusers often use ***isolation*** as a means of control. They may systematically isolate victims from their friends and family, reducing their access to external perspectives and support networks. This isolation creates a heightened dependence on the abuser for emotional support and companionship, making it harder for victims to envision life outside the relationship.

Financial dependency is another significant obstacle. Victims may sometimes rely on their abusers for financial stability, housing, or other resources. The fear of losing these necessities can create a tangible barrier to leaving the relationship, as victims may struggle to find housing or employment independently.

Fear of retaliation looms large for many victims. Abusers often use threats, intimidation, and violence to maintain control, instilling profound fear in their victims. Leaving the relationship can be terrifying, as victims may anticipate escalated abuse or even harm to themselves or their loved ones.

Additionally, victims frequently grapple with ***feelings of shame and stigma***. Society often places blame on the victim, creating a sense of embarrassment and guilt. Victims may feel responsible for the abuse or believe they won't find a better relationship elsewhere, exacerbating their feelings of worthlessness.

Lastly, ***abusers erode their victims' self-esteem and self-worth***, making it challenging to recognize their value and agency. This behavior undermines their belief in their ability to leave the relationship or find a healthier one.

Recognizing abusive behavior and ending an abusive relationship is a complex and highly individual process influenced by many factors. It often requires external support, safety planning, and access to resources for immediate safety and long-term independence. Encouraging victims to seek help and providing non-judgmental support is critical in assisting them on this arduous journey toward safety, healing, and reclaiming their lives.

Chapter 3: Making the Decision to Leave

Many victims of narcissistic abuse in relationships will attempt to leave several times before they are successful. Return to those points at the end of Chapter 2 – the narcissist has broken down all support systems. They have made the person so dependable upon them – financially and emotionally. So even when a person is ready to leave, the first questions will be...

"Where will I go?"

"How will I pay for that?"

"Who can I call?"

"Where do I start?"

The narcissist in the relationship will have successfully broken down many friendships, family, and other supports. A person might find themselves with no independent income and feel they have nowhere to go. In those circumstances, it becomes easier to stay.

In this Chapter, we'll work through important factors to work through as you decide to leave and then stick to it.

Assessing the situation: Evaluating the level of toxicity and abuse

Assessing the situation and evaluating the level of toxicity and abuse is crucial in deciding to leave an abusive relationship.

Here are some key points to consider:

1. **Recognizing Patterns:** Identifying recurring patterns of abusive behavior within the relationship is essential. This includes verbal, emotional, psychological, or physical abuse. Keeping a journal of incidents can help document these patterns and clarify the extent of the abuse.

2. **Assessing Impact:** Consider the impact of the abuse on your physical and emotional well-being. Are you experiencing anxiety, depression, or physical injuries as a result of the relationship? Recognizing the harm caused by the toxicity is a motivating factor to seek change.

3. **Safety Concerns:** Assess your safety within the relationship. Suppose you fear for your safety or the safety of your children. In that case, it's imperative to prioritize immediate safety measures, such as finding a safe place to stay or seeking assistance from a domestic violence shelter or hotline.

4. **Seeking Support:** Contact trusted friends, family members, or professionals who can provide objective perspectives. Discussing the abuse with someone you trust can help you gain insight into the severity of the toxicity and explore options for leaving.

5. **Understanding Control Tactics:** Recognize the various control tactics employed by the abuser, such as isolation, financial control, or manipulation. Understanding how these tactics are used to maintain power and control can empower you to break free from them.

Assessing the level of toxicity and abuse is a critical step in making an informed decision about leaving an abusive relationship. It provides a foundation for creating a safety plan, seeking support, and taking steps to reclaim your life and well-being.

One more thing before we meet our couple for this Chapter. In going through the above assessment, it is important, very important, to make a proper assessment of safety and the level of control exerted by the narcissist. When you make the decision to leave – ***go and go quickly***, gather your things and leave. Avoid a long drawn-out process. Do not put yourself in a position where your safety, or the safety of any children you have, is compromised.

Now, let's meet **Catherine and Beth**.

Catherine and Beth had been in a same-sex relationship for several years, living together in a cozy apartment in a vibrant city. Initially, their love was passionate, and they shared dreams of a future. However, as time passed, Beth began to notice unsettling patterns in their relationship.

Catherine displayed clear signs of narcissistic behavior. She frequently belittled Beth, criticizing her appearance, career choices, and friendships. Catherine often boasted about her accomplishments and belittled Beth's achievements, leaving Beth feeling inadequate and undeserving of love. Catherine also maintained control over their finances, limiting Beth's access to money and making her financially dependent.

The emotional manipulation was relentless. Catherine used guilt-tripping tactics to keep Beth emotionally entangled. Whenever Beth expressed a desire to leave or voiced her concerns about the relationship, Catherine would play the victim, tearfully claiming that Beth was abandoning her or that she couldn't survive without her. These emotional pleas made Beth question her own feelings and created a suffocating sense of obligation.

Isolation was another weapon in Catherine's arsenal. She gradually distanced Beth from her friends and family, making her increasingly dependent on their toxic relationship for companionship and support. Beth's social circle dwindled, leaving her feeling isolated and trapped.

As Beth grappled with the decision to leave, she faced numerous obstacles. Her self-esteem had been eroded over time, making her believe she deserved the mistreatment. She felt ashamed to admit the true nature of her relationship to friends and family, fearing judgment and rejection. The fear of Catherine's retaliation and the uncertain future without her made the decision to leave an emotionally daunting one.

Beth knew that leaving would not be easy, but she also recognized that it was necessary for her well-being. She secretly reached out to a local support group for survivors of abusive relationships, where she found the encouragement and resources she needed to take the first steps toward reclaiming her life.

This scenario illustrates the complexities of leaving a toxic same-sex relationship where narcissistic behavior is present. It highlights abuse victims' emotional and psychological challenges and the importance of seeking support and resources to break free from such harmful dynamics.

Overcoming guilt and fear associated with leaving a narcissist

Overcoming the guilt and fear associated with leaving a narcissist is an arduous yet essential journey toward reclaiming one's life and well-being. In a relationship with a narcissist, feelings of guilt and fear are often deliberately cultivated and exploited by the abuser as tools of control. Here, we look at ways individuals can break free from these emotional shackles and move toward a healthier, happier future.

Guilt is a common emotion experienced by those contemplating leaving a narcissistic relationship. The narcissist skillfully manipulates their victim's emotions, often portraying themselves as the victim or unfairly blaming the victim for any issues in the relationship. Victims feel responsible for the narcissist's emotional well-being, even though it's entirely unfounded. **Understanding that this guilt is a product of manipulation**, not a reflection of reality, is a crucial first step.

Fear, another powerful emotion, often keeps victims trapped in narcissistic relationships. The fear of retaliation, violence, or the unknown can be paralyzing. Narcissists may use threats, intimidation, or financial control to maintain power over their victims, amplifying these fears. It's essential to acknowledge and validate these fears but not allow them to dictate one's choices.

Recovery from a narcissistic relationship is a complex process that often requires professional assistance. **Therapists, counselors, and support groups** specializing in abuse recovery can provide invaluable guidance and a safe space to explore and address feelings of guilt and fear. These professionals can help individuals understand the dynamics of narcissistic abuse, validate their experiences, and develop coping strategies.

Narcissists excel at eroding their victims' self-esteem. To overcome guilt and fear, individuals must embark on **self-healing and self-discovery**. This journey involves rebuilding self-esteem and self-worth, recognizing their own value as individuals deserving of love, respect, and happiness.

Fear of retaliation is a valid concern when leaving a narcissistic relationship. **Creating a safety plan** that includes securing a safe place to stay, contacting local support agencies or domestic violence hotlines, and involving law enforcement, if necessary, can mitigate these fears. Having a concrete plan in place helps individuals regain a sense of control over their lives.

Building a **support system** is crucial for overcoming guilt and fear. Sharing one's experiences with trusted friends and family can provide validation and emotional support. Connecting with others who have experienced similar situations through support groups or online communities can be empowering and reassuring.

Minimizing contact with the narcissist can help alleviate both guilt and fear. Going **no-contact**, if possible, can break the cycle of manipulation and control, allowing for emotional healing. In cases where complete separation isn't feasible, maintaining **low contact** and implementing strict boundaries is vital for self-preservation.

Knowledge is a potent weapon against guilt and fear. Learning about narcissistic personality disorder, abusive tactics, and the dynamics of abusive relationships can provide individuals with clarity and validation. It helps to understand that the narcissist's behavior is not their fault and that leaving is necessary for self-preservation.

Overcoming guilt and fear associated with leaving a narcissist is an ongoing process. It requires patience, self-compassion, and a commitment to one's own well-being. It's essential to remember that healing is possible, and there is a brighter future beyond the shadows of a narcissistic relationship.

In the context of Beth leaving Catherine, there are several crucial steps and support measures that Beth should consider:

1. **Reach Out to a Support Network:** Beth should confide in trusted friends and family members who can provide emotional support and understanding. These individuals can offer a safe space to express their feelings and concerns, validate their experiences, and provide practical assistance.

2. **Seek Professional Help:** Consulting a therapist or counselor specializing in narcissistic abuse and LGBTQ+ issues can be immensely beneficial. A therapist can help Beth navigate the complexities of leaving and healing from the abusive relationship. They can provide guidance on setting boundaries, managing emotions, and rebuilding self-esteem.

3. **Safety Planning:** Beth should create a safety plan to ensure her physical and emotional well-being while leaving Catherine. This plan may involve identifying a safe place to stay, securing important documents, and having an emergency contact list readily available. It's essential to prioritize safety above all else.

4. **Contact Support Organizations:** Research and reach out to local or national organizations that specialize in supporting survivors of abusive relationships within the LGBTQ+ community. These organizations often offer resources, legal assistance, and guidance on leaving abusive situations.

5. **Legal Protection:** If necessary, consult with a lawyer who has experience with LGBTQ+ family law and can help Beth understand her rights and legal options. This process may

include obtaining restraining orders or custody arrangements if children are involved.

6. ***Financial Independence:*** Work on achieving financial independence if Catherine controlled the finances during their relationship. Steps here may involve opening a separate bank account, securing a source of income, or seeking financial counseling to regain control over her finances.

7. ***Self-Care:*** Prioritize self-care and self-compassion throughout the process of leaving and healing. While it may feel like an indulgence, practicing self-love and engaging in activities that bring joy and fulfillment are essential steps to rebuild Beth's self-esteem.

Leaving an abusive relationship with a narcissistic partner is a challenging journey, but with the right support and resources, Beth can regain control of her life, heal from the trauma, and move towards a healthier and happier future.

Creating a support system: Family, friends, and professional resources

Creating a support system encompassing family, friends, and professional resources is an imperative and foundational step when leaving an abusive relationship, particularly one characterized by isolation. The isolation orchestrated by narcissistic abusers is a potent weapon used to exert control over their victims. By isolating them from their social circles, friends, and even family, the abuser creates an environment where the victim becomes emotionally and socially dependent solely on them. In such a distorted reality, victims may lose touch with their own perceptions, doubt their self-worth, and feel trapped in the cycle of abuse. This is precisely why establishing a robust support system becomes a lifeline for those seeking to break free from the clutches of an abusive relationship.

One of the primary roles of a support system is to **counteract the effects of isolation**. Family, friends, and professional resources reintroduce healthy social connections and breathe fresh air into the victim's life. Trusted individuals can serve as a beacon of hope, guiding victims out of the dark and tumultuous waters of abuse. These supporters provide a critical anchor to reality, validating the victim's experiences. Victims often endure gaslighting, a manipulative tactic employed by narcissistic abusers to make them doubt their own perceptions and memories. In this context, the support system becomes a source of validation, confirming that the victim's feelings and experiences are real and deserving of attention.

Furthermore, **friends and family can provide a reality check**, offering an objective perspective on the abusive relationship. This external viewpoint is invaluable because, over time, the abuser may have convinced the victim that the abuse is normal or deserved. A support system can help victims reestablish a sense of self and regain the self-confidence the abuser systematically eroded.

Emotionally, leaving an abusive relationship is an overwhelming journey. Feelings of loneliness, despair, and self-doubt can be pervasive. This is where the emotional support provided by a support system comes into play. **Friends and family can lend a listening ear**, offer comfort during difficult moments, and provide a safe space for the victim to express their feelings. Knowing that there are people who care and believe in their strength and resilience can be a powerful motivator to take the necessary steps to leave the abusive relationship.

Practical support is equally essential. Professionals, such as therapists and counselors specializing in abuse recovery, can assist victims in creating safety plans tailored to their unique situations. These plans encompass immediate safety and long-term well-being strategies, addressing concerns like housing, finances, and legal matters. In many cases, the victim may fear retaliation or escalating abuse upon leaving, so a safety plan is crucial for ensuring physical and emotional safety.

A support system also connects victims with **essential resources**. This includes domestic violence hotlines, shelters, legal aid services, and support groups. These resources offer critical guidance and assistance for safety and recovery. They help victims navigate the practical aspects of leaving an abusive relationship, such as finding safe housing, securing financial independence, or pursuing legal action if necessary.

Moreover, the presence of a support system **empowers victims**. Interactions with supportive individuals boost self-esteem and self-worth, which are often severely damaged by the abuse. Knowing that they have people in their corner who believe in their strength and resilience can be a catalyst for change. It can empower victims to take the necessary steps to leave the abusive relationship, breaking free from the cycle of control and manipulation.

Additionally, ***a support system is a protective buffer***, reducing the victim's vulnerability to manipulation and control. The abuser often employs tactics to isolate the victim and keep them under their influence. However, with a support system, victims have a protective shield that deters the abuser from escalating abusive behaviors, as they know their tactics are less likely to succeed.

Finally, ***leaving an abusive relationship is just the beginning of the healing process***. The aftermath of abuse can leave lasting emotional scars. A strong support system offers ongoing support and guidance during the recovery journey. Friends and family can provide emotional support, understanding, and encouragement as victims work to rebuild their lives. Additionally, professional resources, such as therapy and support groups, can help victims process their trauma, learn healthy coping mechanisms, and develop a more profound sense of self-worth.

Creating a support system is a critical step and a lifeline for individuals leaving abusive relationships, especially when isolation is a significant factor. It serves as a bridge from the darkness of abuse to the promise of a brighter future. It offers validation, emotional support, practical assistance, and empowerment. It helps victims break free from the cycle of abuse, regain their autonomy, and embark on a path toward healing and a life filled with safety, self-love, and resilience.

Developing a safety plan and establishing boundaries

Developing a safety plan and establishing boundaries are paramount when leaving an abusive relationship, as they are essential for ensuring the victim's safety, both physically and emotionally. A safety plan is a strategic approach to navigating the challenging process of leaving, while boundaries serve as protective barriers against further manipulation and control.

A safety plan involves **identifying potential risks and preparing for contingencies**. It includes steps like securing a safe place to stay, such as a domestic violence shelter, or with supportive friends or family members, as leaving can escalate tension and put the victim at risk of harm. It may also encompass securing essential documents, like identification and financial records, to maintain autonomy and independence. A safety plan considers how to handle communication with the abuser, whether it's through no-contact or low-contact strategies to minimize potential confrontation. Victims should have an emergency contact list, including law enforcement and support agencies, readily accessible. Safety planning is a dynamic process that adapts to the victim's specific circumstances and evolves as they progress toward leaving the relationship.

Establishing boundaries is crucial for reclaiming autonomy and protecting against further abuse. Boundaries define what behavior is acceptable and what is not, providing a clear framework for interaction. Victims of narcissistic abuse often experience blurred boundaries as the abuser seeks to control and manipulate every aspect of their lives. Setting boundaries involves clearly communicating expectations and limits to the abuser and enforcing consequences for violations. This can include blocking communication, limiting access to personal information, and refusing to engage in confrontations or arguments. Boundaries also extend to interactions with friends and family who may have been manipulated or coerced by the abuser; victims can establish boundaries to protect their own emotional well-being and ensure they receive the support they need.

Developing a safety plan and establishing boundaries require careful consideration and guidance. It is advisable to **consult with professionals** specializing in domestic violence and abuse recovery, such as therapists or counselors, to create a personalized safety plan and receive guidance on boundary-setting. Additionally, support groups for abuse survivors can provide insight and practical strategies for safety planning and boundary establishment. Ultimately, these measures are vital for ensuring victims can leave the abusive relationship with more security, autonomy, and protection from further harm.

In Beth and Catherine's relationship and Beth's heightened fear due to Catherine's extreme behaviors, safety planning becomes critical and urgent for Beth's well-being. Consider this dynamic in Beth's situation and the steps she must take to ensure her safety:

Beth had reached a breaking point in her tumultuous relationship with Catherine, whose extreme narcissistic behaviors had escalated alarmingly. Catherine's unpredictable rages, threats, and acts of aggression had instilled an overwhelming fear in Beth. She knew that leaving this abusive relationship was no longer a choice but an imperative for her safety and sanity.

Beth understood that her safety plan needed to **address the immediate threats** posed by Catherine's extreme behaviors. She acknowledged that Catherine's actions had become increasingly unpredictable, and any attempt to leave might trigger an explosive response. She took stock of the most dangerous situations and behaviors that Catherine exhibited, including physical violence, property damage, and stalking.

Beth's first step in her safety plan was to **secure a safe place to stay**. She contacted a local domestic violence shelter and arranged for temporary accommodation. This ensured that she had a secure and undisclosed location where Catherine could not locate her.

Beth was aware that she might need the **involvement of law enforcement** to ensure her safety. She documented instances of Catherine's extreme behaviors, including photographs of damaged property and threatening messages. She had the local police department's non-emergency number saved in her phone and knew the procedure for obtaining a restraining order if necessary.

Beth took immediate steps to **restrict contact** with Catherine. She changed her phone number and blocked Catherine on all social media and email accounts. She informed her workplace about the situation, providing them with Catherine's photograph and description to prevent any unwelcome visits or harassment.

Beth packed an **emergency bag** containing essentials such as identification, important documents, medications, and a change of clothes. She kept this bag hidden at her safe location, ready to grab in case she needed to leave quickly.

Beth **confided in a few close friends and family members** about her situation. She shared her safety plan with them, providing them with her safe location's address and contact information. These trusted contacts served as her lifeline, ready to assist if Catherine attempted to interfere with her escape.

Beth **consulted with a lawyer** experienced in domestic violence cases to explore legal options, including obtaining a restraining order or an emergency custody order if applicable. She documented Catherine's extreme behaviors and any threats made, ensuring she had a strong case if legal action became necessary.

Recognizing the emotional toll of Catherine's extreme behaviors, Beth sought **therapeutic support** from a counselor experienced in trauma and abuse recovery. Therapy sessions helped her cope with the fear and anxiety that had taken a toll on her mental health.

Beth's safety planning was an ongoing process, adapting to the ever-evolving circumstances created by Catherine's extreme behaviors. It was a lifeline, meticulously crafted to ensure her safety, autonomy, and freedom from the oppressive grip of an abusive relationship. As she took these steps, Beth moved toward a future where she could regain control of her life and heal from the trauma of Catherine's extreme narcissistic behaviors.

Gathering evidence and preparing for legal proceedings

Gathering evidence and preparing for legal proceedings is paramount when leaving an abusive relationship, particularly one involving extreme narcissistic behaviors. This crucial step serves several vital purposes, ultimately safeguarding the victim's rights and well-being.

Firstly, gathering evidence **bolsters the victim's case and credibility in legal proceedings**. In situations where the abuser has exhibited extreme behaviors, such as threats, physical violence, or harassment, documented evidence is a compelling testament to the victim's claims. It can establish a pattern of abusive conduct, strengthening the case for restraining orders, custody arrangements, or other legal remedies.

Secondly, evidence collection is a ***proactive measure to ensure the victim's safety***. It provides law enforcement and legal authorities with a clear picture of the extent of the abuse, which can expedite the issuance of protective orders. The presence of documented evidence can deter the abuser from escalating their behaviors or retaliating against the victim, as they know the potential legal consequences.

Moreover, ***evidence can play a pivotal role in child custody cases***. In situations where children are involved, courts consider the safety and well-being of the child as the highest priority. Gathering evidence of the abuser's extreme behaviors, especially if they threaten the child's safety, can be instrumental in securing a custody arrangement that protects the child and the victim.

Additionally, evidence collection is an ***essential component of accountability***. It holds the abuser responsible for their actions and can lead to legal repercussions, such as criminal charges or mandated counseling and anger management programs. This accountability can contribute to breaking the cycle of abuse and preventing future harm to the victim or others.

Lastly, gathering evidence ***empowers the victim*** by providing them with a sense of agency and control over their situation. It shifts the balance of power away from the abuser and towards the victim's pursuit of justice and safety. It also demonstrates to the victim that their experiences are valid and deserving of legal protection.

Gathering evidence and preparing for legal proceedings is vital when leaving an abusive relationship characterized by extreme narcissistic behaviors. It bolsters the victim's legal case and serves as a means of protection, accountability, and empowerment. By documenting the abuse and ensuring that it is legally addressed, victims can take significant steps towards breaking free from the cycle of abuse and securing a safer and healthier future.

However, and this is important, ***do not prioritize gathering your evidence over your own safety***. If your safety, or the safety of any children you have, is at risk – leave the evidence and go.

What about the kids?

Before we leave this topic, let's consider how Beth and Catherine's scenario might change if they had a child, Sara, who is five years old. Here, the overall dynamics of leaving the abusive relationship would become significantly more complex and sensitive.

Safety Planning:

1. **Child's Safety:** The safety and well-being of Sara would become the highest priority. Beth must ensure that Sara is protected from witnessing or experiencing abuse. This may involve finding a safe place for Sara and Beth to stay, such as a domestic violence shelter or with trusted family members.

2. **Custody Arrangements:** Leaving the abusive relationship with Sara would entail addressing custody arrangements. Beth would need to consult with a lawyer to establish a custody plan

that prioritizes Sara's safety and minimizes her exposure to Catherine's extreme behaviors.

3. **Communication:** Managing communication with Catherine, especially regarding Sara, would require careful consideration. Beth may need to establish boundaries and utilize third-party communication methods, such as a co-parenting app or mediator, to ensure that Sara's needs are met without exposing Beth to further abuse.

Legal Proceedings:

1. **Child Custody Proceedings:** Legal proceedings would likely include child custody hearings where the court evaluates the best interests of Sara. Evidence of Catherine's extreme behaviors and their potential impact on Sara's well-being would be crucial in determining custody arrangements.

2. **Protective Orders:** Beth may seek protective orders for herself and Sara, ensuring that Catherine is legally prohibited from approaching or contacting them.

3. **Supervised Visitation:** Depending on the severity of Catherine's behaviors, the court may order supervised visitation, where Sara's interactions with Catherine are closely monitored to ensure her safety.

Overall Dynamics:

1. **Child's Emotional Well-Being:** Beth and Sara would require emotional support to cope with their traumatic experiences. Sara's emotional well-being, in particular, would be a primary

concern, and therapy or counseling may be necessary for both mother and child.

2. **Education and Explanation:** Beth would need to find age-appropriate ways to explain the situation to Sara, ensuring she understands that leaving is for their safety without causing unnecessary fear or confusion.

3. **Co-Parenting Challenges:** Co-parenting with an abusive ex-partner becomes especially challenging when a child is involved. Beth and Catherine may need to navigate complex dynamics while prioritizing Sara's stability and emotional health.

In summary, having a child significantly complicates leaving an abusive relationship characterized by extreme narcissistic behaviors. The child's safety, well-being, and emotional health become paramount, influencing safety planning, legal proceedings, and overall family dynamics. It is essential to seek professional guidance and legal advice to navigate these complex situations and protect the child's best interests.

What to Do if Your Friends and Family Don't Understand

Navigating the challenges of leaving an abusive relationship, especially one marked by extreme narcissistic behaviors, can be arduous. Yet, what can be equally challenging is finding that your friends and family may not fully understand or support your decision to leave. In such situations, knowing what steps to take and how to manage judgment and others' expectations is essential.

If your loved ones struggle to comprehend your decision to leave, consider **seeking the assistance of a therapist or counselor** specializing in abusive relationships. They can provide valuable insights and information to help your friends and family better understand the complexities of narcissistic abuse.

Provide resources and literature on narcissistic abuse to your friends and family. Sharing articles, books, or videos explaining the dynamics of abusive relationships can shed light on why leaving is often the best choice for safety and well-being.

Communicate your boundaries to your loved ones regarding discussions about your abusive relationship. Let them know what you are comfortable sharing and what topics are off-limits. This can help minimize judgment and unnecessary interference.

Connect with support groups or online communities of survivors who have experienced similar challenges. These groups can offer empathy, advice, and a sense of belonging, as members have likely encountered friends and family who don't understand their choices.

Understand that *it may take time* for your friends and family to grasp the gravity of your situation. People often need time to process complex information and adjust their perspectives. Be patient and allow them the opportunity to learn and grow in their understanding.

Remember that *your safety and well-being are paramount*. Your decision to leave is based on the need to protect yourself from harm. Stay focused on your goals and prioritize your mental and physical health.

Be kind to yourself and recognize that you are making a courageous and necessary choice. Self-doubt and guilt may arise when facing judgment, but it's essential to remind yourself that you are taking steps toward a safer and healthier future.

Understand that you may not be able to change others' opinions or expectations overnight. ***Set realistic expectations***. Focus on what you can control, which is your own path to healing and recovery.

Surround yourself with supportive individuals. Seek out friends, family members, or support groups who understand and support your decision to leave. Building a network of people who validate your experiences and choices can provide the emotional bolstering you need.

If certain individuals continue to be judgmental or unsupportive, consider limiting your contact with them, at least temporarily. ***Surrounding yourself with positivity*** and support can help you regain strength and confidence.

Facing judgment and a lack of understanding from friends and family when leaving an abusive relationship can be disheartening. However, you can navigate these challenges by educating your loved ones, setting boundaries, seeking professional guidance, and prioritizing your well-being while staying true to your path to safety and healing. Remember that your decision to leave is a courageous step toward reclaiming your life, and you deserve understanding and support on your journey to recovery.

Chapter 4: Navigating the Legal Process

In the turbulent journey of divorcing a narcissistic partner, one of the most formidable challenges is navigating the legal process. This chapter serves as a guiding compass, offering insights, strategies, and a roadmap for those embarking on this complex and often emotionally charged journey.

Divorce, under any circumstances, can be a labyrinthine legal endeavor. When a narcissistic partner is involved, the complexities can escalate exponentially. Their relentless need for control, manipulation, and desire to "win" at all costs can turn the divorce proceedings into a battleground.

Divorcing a narcissist can be emotionally draining, and their tactics can be confounding. This chapter provides clarity and guidance, addressing common legal challenges and offering practical steps to protect your rights and interests. It emphasizes the importance of self-advocacy and resilience in the face of adversity.

As you embark on this chapter's journey, remember you are not alone. Many have walked this path before, and their experiences and wisdom have paved the way for your own empowerment. With the proper knowledge and support, you can navigate the legal process with determination, ensuring your voice is heard and your rights are protected.

Before we go further into this chapter, let's meet **Lucy and Christopher**.

Lucy and Christopher's relationship had once promised a bright and loving future. They met during their college years, drawn to each other's passion for art, and shared dreams of a life filled with creativity and adventure. However, as the years passed, the idyllic picture began to fade, revealing a darker reality.

Once charismatic and charming, Christopher had transformed into a person consumed by his own desires and ambitions. His grandiose sense of self-importance had spiraled into aggressive and controlling behavior. He frequently belittled Lucy's dreams, dismissing her artistic pursuits as insignificant compared to his own. Their arguments became increasingly heated, escalating into episodes of violence, leaving Lucy emotionally and physically scarred.

Christopher's need for dominance extended beyond their home, infiltrating their social circle. He insisted on being the center of attention, monopolizing conversations, and portraying himself as the victim when confronted about his abusive behavior.

Once full of life and creativity, Lucy had become trapped in a nightmarish existence. She lived in constant fear of Christopher's temper and the next explosive outburst. Her self-esteem was eroded, leaving her feeling powerless and voiceless.

As the relationship reached its breaking point, Lucy began seeking a way out, driven by the hope of reclaiming her life and finding the strength to overcome the toxic grip of Christopher's narcissistic and abusive behavior.

Securing legal representation experienced in dealing with narcissistic partners

Securing legal representation while divorcing a narcissistic partner is a pivotal step toward liberation and justice. The complexities of such divorces, marked by manipulation, control, and emotional volatility, necessitate not only legal expertise but also a profound understanding of the unique challenges posed by narcissistic individuals. This section delves into the critical aspects of finding the right lawyer and highlights the added consideration of choosing legal representation experienced in dealing with narcissistic partners.

Divorcing a narcissistic partner often involves navigating a legal battleground where power dynamics are skewed, and emotions run high. To successfully protect your rights and interests, it is imperative to **engage a lawyer who specializes in family law** and has a deep comprehension of the intricate dynamics at play. Such a lawyer can provide guidance on the legal process and offer strategic counsel tailored to the specific challenges a narcissistic spouse poses.

One of the foremost considerations when selecting legal representation is *experience*. A lawyer who has previously handled divorces involving narcissistic partners brings valuable insights. They are well-versed in the manipulation tactics, deceitful behaviors, and emotional turbulence often exhibited by narcissists during divorce proceedings. This experience equips them with the ability to anticipate the strategies employed by the opposing party and develop countermeasures to protect your rights effectively.

Communication is another critical aspect of legal representation when dealing with a narcissistic partner. Your lawyer should be a strong and assertive communicator who can effectively advocate for your interests while maintaining professional composure in the face of manipulation or aggression. They can act as a buffer between you and your ex-spouse, minimizing direct contact and reducing the potential for further conflict.

When discussing your case with a potential lawyer, ask about their experience handling divorces involving narcissistic partners. Inquire about their success stories, strategies employed, and their understanding of the emotional toll such divorces can take. Subject to confidentiality requirements, a skilled lawyer may be able to provide ***references or testimonials*** from clients who have faced similar challenges and achieved favorable outcomes.

Ultimately, securing legal representation experienced in dealing with narcissistic partners is not merely an option but a strategic necessity. It ensures that you have an advocate who understands the nuances of these high-conflict divorces and can guide you through the legal process with empathy and expertise. With the right lawyer, you are better equipped to navigate the turbulent waters of divorcing a narcissistic partner, ultimately moving closer to a future of empowerment, freedom, and emotional healing.

Finding the most suitable lawyer in Lucy's case is crucial for her well-being and success in the legal process. Lucy should:

1. **Seek Recommendations and Conduct Research:** Lucy can start her search by seeking recommendations from trusted sources, such as friends, family members, or support groups for

survivors of narcissistic abuse. These recommendations often come with valuable insights and personal experiences. Additionally, Lucy should conduct thorough online research to identify lawyers with expertise in family law and experience handling cases involving narcissistic spouses. Reading client reviews and testimonials can provide further insight into a lawyer's track record and client satisfaction.

2. **Interview Multiple Lawyers:** Lucy should schedule initial consultations with several lawyers to gauge their suitability for her case. During these interviews, she should ask pertinent questions, such as:

- "Have you handled divorce cases involving narcissistic or abusive spouses before?"

- "What strategies do you employ to protect clients from manipulation and emotional abuse during divorce proceedings?"

- "Can you provide references from clients who have faced similar situations?"

The key is to assess the lawyer's knowledge, experience, and communication style. Lucy should also evaluate how comfortable she feels discussing her situation with the lawyer, as trust and open communication are essential.

3. **Consider Specialized Support:** Given the unique challenges posed by narcissistic partners, Lucy may benefit from seeking a lawyer specializing in high-conflict divorces or has experience

dealing with personality disorders. These lawyers are often better equipped to understand and navigate the complexities of such cases. Lucy can also explore collaborative divorce or mediation options, which may help reduce conflict and provide a more controlled negotiation environment. When Lucy has experienced physical violence from Christopher, it will be necessary that any power imbalance or safety concerns are catered for.

In addition to these tips, Lucy should prioritize her emotional well-being throughout the process. She may want to engage in therapy or support groups to help cope with the emotional toll of divorcing a narcissistic and abusive partner. Building a solid support network of friends and family can also provide invaluable emotional support during this challenging time. With the right legal representation and emotional support, Lucy can embark on her journey toward liberation and healing.

Gathering evidence and presenting a strong case

One of the primary reasons for gathering evidence is to **safeguard one's legal rights**. There are complex issues to address in any divorce, including property division, spousal support, child custody, and visitation. Failing to present a strong case can result in unfair or unfavorable outcomes, leaving one at a significant disadvantage. Compelling evidence can substantiate claims, support arguments, and ensure the final divorce decree aligns with legal entitlements.

When children are involved, their best interests must take precedence. Gathering evidence related to a **child's safety, well-being, and** *relationship* with each parent is essential. This includes documenting instances of neglect, abuse, or any actions that may threaten the child's physical or emotional health. Courts rely heavily on evidence to make informed decisions regarding custody arrangements, visitation schedules, and child support, aiming to create a stable and nurturing environment for the children.

Narcissistic or contentious partners often employ manipulation tactics, including deceit, false allegations, and gaslighting, to shape the narrative in their favor. ***Collecting tangible evidence*** counters these tactics and ensures that the truth prevails. It can discredit false claims, reveal statement inconsistencies, and expose attempts to distort the facts.

Narcissistic partners may exhibit a pattern of abusive or problematic behavior over time. Gathering evidence allows for ***documenting this pattern***, highlighting recurrent issues such as emotional abuse, financial misconduct, or a history of aggression. Demonstrating a consistent pattern can be instrumental in persuading the court to make decisions that protect the victim's rights and well-being.

Even if divorce proceedings do not go to trial, evidence plays a ***vital role in negotiation and settlement discussions***. It can provide leverage during negotiations, prompting the opposing party to consider a fairer settlement to avoid the risks and expenses associated with a trial. Substantial evidence can lead to more amicable and mutually beneficial resolutions.

In abusive or illegal behavior cases, evidence can have ***legal consequences beyond divorce*** proceedings. It may support criminal charges, restraining orders, or other legal actions against the abusive partner. This can lead to protection for the victim and accountability for the aggressor.

Finally, gathering evidence and presenting a strong case can give the victim **closure and justice**. It acknowledges the suffering endured and offers a path toward healing and moving forward. Knowing that the truth has been recognized and upheld can bring peace of mind and a fresh start to life after divorce.

In Lucy's case, one of the most effective ways to build a strong case is through meticulous documentation. Lucy should keep a detailed record of all interactions, incidents of abuse, threats, and any concerning behavior exhibited by Christopher. This includes saving text messages, emails, voicemails, and social media posts as evidence of his behavior. She should also document any physical abuse, injuries, or damages caused during altercations. Keeping a journal to record these incidents' dates, times, locations, and witnesses can be invaluable.

Lucy should gather all financial records, including bank statements, tax returns, credit card statements, and documentation of any joint assets or debts. This will help ensure a fair division of assets and liabilities and can be crucial if Christopher attempts to hide or manipulate financial information.

If Christopher controls the finances and manages all documentation, Lucy may face significant challenges in gathering evidence for her divorce case. Lucy should consult with an experienced family lawyer immediately. A knowledgeable lawyer can guide legal avenues to access financial information, such as subpoenas, depositions, or requests for the production of documents. They can also advise on navigating the specific laws and regulations governing financial disclosure in divorce cases.

Throughout this process, Lucy must remain calm and composed, especially during interactions with Christopher. Narcissistic partners often attempt to provoke emotional reactions, and Christopher may try to use any evidence of erratic behavior against her. Lucy can present herself as a credible and reliable witness by staying focused on the legal proceedings and maintaining her composure.

Managing Court Proceedings and Potential Challenges

Managing court proceedings in divorce cases involving a narcissistic or contentious partner presents a myriad of challenges and complexities. These challenges can encompass legal, emotional, and practical aspects, making the process both demanding and emotionally draining. Here, we explore some potential challenges that can arise when navigating court proceedings in such cases.

Divorcing a narcissistic partner often means engaging in **high-conflict proceedings**. These partners thrive on confrontation and may employ aggressive legal tactics to intimidate or overwhelm the other party. This heightened conflict can escalate tensions and prolong the legal process, increasing emotional distress for both parties.

Narcissistic partners are **adept at manipulation**, both inside and outside the courtroom. They may attempt to use legal maneuvers to control the narrative or delay proceedings. Common tactics include false allegations, frivolous motions, and attempts to undermine the other party's credibility. Managing these manipulative strategies requires a strategic and resilient legal approach.

Court proceedings can be **emotionally draining**, particularly for the victim of narcissistic abuse. Facing an abusive partner in court, reliving traumatic experiences, and enduring character attacks can take a severe emotional toll. Managing these emotions and maintaining composure during proceedings can be a significant challenge.

In cases involving children, co-parenting disputes often arise. Narcissistic partners may **use custody battles to maintain control or punish** the other party. Balancing the children's best interests with the need for protection from the abusive parent can be a delicate and emotionally charged challenge.

High-conflict court proceedings can result in **substantial legal costs**. The narcissistic partner's aggressive tactics may lead to protracted litigation, increasing lawyer fees and court expenses. Managing these costs while pursuing a just resolution can be financially burdensome.

Narcissistic individuals may exhibit **disruptive or combative behavior** in court. Their attempts to manipulate proceedings or intimidate the other party can create a hostile environment. Managing courtroom behavior and ensuring a fair and respectful atmosphere can be challenging.

Narcissistic partners may **attempt to discredit the victim** by distorting facts or launching personal attacks. Their goal is often to undermine the victim's credibility and credibility in the eyes of the court. Effective legal representation is crucial to counteract these tactics and present a compelling case.

Enforcing court orders, such as restraining orders or custody arrangements, can be challenging when *dealing with a non-compliant narcissistic partner*. They may disregard court directives, requiring additional legal action to ensure compliance.

The victim's *safety concerns* must be addressed in physical or emotional abuse cases. Ensuring the safety of the victim and any children involved is paramount. This may include securing protective orders and coordinating with law enforcement when necessary.

The journey toward emotional healing and recovery continues even after court proceedings. In the *post-divorce recovery phase*, the victim may grapple with the lingering effects of abuse, trauma, and the need to rebuild their life and self-esteem.

Managing court proceedings with a narcissistic partner in divorce demands resilience, strategic planning, and effective legal representation. While these challenges can be formidable, they are not insurmountable. With the right support, resources, and a clear understanding of the complexities involved, individuals can navigate the legal process, protect their rights, and move toward a future free from the toxic influence of their narcissistic ex-partner.

Let's check in with Lucy. Support during court proceedings, especially in challenging situations like Lucy's divorce from Christopher, is crucial for her emotional well-being and legal success.

It is essential that Lucy:

- Hires an experienced family lawyer;

- Has a strong support system in place from friends and family;

- Engages in therapy or counseling to help manage the emotional toll of the divorce proceedings;

- Establishes boundaries to minimize emotional manipulation or distressing interactions with Christopher;

- Documents everything;

- Looks after herself – exercise, a good diet, and adequate sleep all go towards helping Lucy be the best she can be in and outside the courtroom.

Navigating court proceedings when divorcing a narcissistic partner is challenging, but with the right support network and professional guidance, Lucy can endure the process and work toward a more peaceful and empowered future. The key is to prioritize self-care, surround herself with understanding individuals, and focus on her well-being and long-term goals.

Coping with the financial aspects of divorce

Divorce often involves complex financial considerations that individuals need to address to ensure a fair and equitable outcome. Some of the key financial aspects that people generally need to consider in divorce include:

1. **Property Division:** Determining how marital assets and debts will be divided can be challenging. This includes real estate,

investments, retirement accounts, bank accounts, loans, and personal property. The division may be based on community property laws, equitable distribution principles, or specific agreements between the parties. It will depend on what the law is where you live.

2. **Spousal Support:** Spousal support, also known as alimony or maintenance, may be awarded to one spouse to provide financial assistance during and after divorce. The amount and duration of spousal support depend on factors such as the length of the marriage, financial need, and each spouse's earning capacity. It will also depend on what the law is where you live.

3. **Child Support:** Child support is typically calculated based on state guidelines (and differs depending on where you live) and is designed to provide financial support for the children's needs, including education, healthcare, and living expenses. The non-custodial parent usually pays child support to the custodial parent.

4. **Tax Implications:** Divorce can have significant tax consequences. Considerations include filing status, dependency exemptions, tax credits, and the treatment of property transfers. Understanding how divorce will impact your tax situation is essential, and planning accordingly is critical. Tax laws differ in each jurisdiction.

5. **Health Insurance:** Changes in health insurance coverage often accompany divorce. Understanding how health insurance for spouses and dependents will be handled after divorce is essential.

6. **Budgeting and Financial Planning:** Divorce can lead to income, expenses, and lifestyle changes. Developing a post-divorce budget and financial plan is vital to financial stability and long-term goals.

7. **Legal Fees and Court Costs:** Legal representation and court-related expenses can be significant during a divorce. Understanding the costs associated with legal proceedings is essential for financial planning.

Navigating these financial aspects of divorce requires careful planning, professional consultation, and a clear understanding of the legal and financial implications. If necessary, consulting with an experienced family lawyer and financial experts can help individuals make informed decisions and protect their financial interests during divorce.

Paying for a lawyer

Paying for a lawyer in a divorce case is a significant financial consideration, and individuals often have several options to explore:

1. **Retainer Fee:** Many divorce lawyers require clients to pay a retainer fee upfront. The lawyer holds this initial lump sum in a trust account and bills against it as they work on the case. The retainer fee can vary widely based on the case's complexity, location, and the lawyer's experience.

2. **Hourly Billing:** Lawyers typically charge clients on an hourly basis for their services. Clients are billed for the lawyer's time spent on tasks related to the divorce, such as meetings, phone calls, research, drafting legal documents, and court appearances.

Rates can vary widely depending on the lawyer's experience and geographic location.

3. **Flat-Fee Arrangement:** Some lawyers offer flat-fee arrangements for specific divorce services, such as uncontested divorces or drafting settlement agreements. Flat fees provide cost predictability for clients.

4. **Limited-Scope Representation:** In some cases, individuals may choose limited-scope representation, where they hire a lawyer for specific tasks or consultations rather than full representation throughout the divorce process. This can be a more cost-effective option for those with budget constraints.

5. **Consultations and Advice:** Some individuals may opt for a one-time consultation with a lawyer to obtain legal advice and guidance on their divorce case. This can be affordable to get professional insights without committing to full legal representation.

6. **Legal Aid and Pro Bono Services:** Low-income individuals may qualify for free or low-cost legal services through legal aid organizations or pro bono programs offered by law firms. These services are typically income-based and can provide essential legal assistance to those in need.

7. **Mediation:** Mediation is an alternative dispute resolution process where a neutral third party helps couples reach agreements outside of court. The costs are typically shared between both parties.

8. **Collaborative Divorce:** Collaborative divorce involves each spouse hiring a lawyer specializing in collaborative law. The process is designed to be cooperative and less adversarial, which can lead to cost savings compared to litigation.

When considering how to pay for a lawyer, it's essential to:

- **Budget Accordingly:** Create a budget for legal fees, court costs, and other related expenses. Understand the financial commitment required for your divorce case.

- **Explore Payment Plans:** Some lawyers may offer payment plans to help clients manage legal fees over time. Discuss payment options with potential lawyers.

- **Negotiate Fees:** Sometimes, individuals can negotiate legal fees with their lawyer. Be open to discussing fee structures and finding an arrangement that works for both parties.

- **Do Not Underestimate the Value of Legal Representation:** While legal fees can be a significant expense, the value of having an experienced lawyer who can protect your rights and interests during the divorce process is often well worth the investment.

Choosing a lawyer who aligns with your financial situation and goals is crucial. Consulting with multiple lawyers, comparing their fee structures, and discussing your budget and expectations upfront can help you decide how to pay for legal representation during your divorce.

Navigating the legal divorce process is undeniably challenging, especially when dealing with a narcissistic or high-conflict partner. However, with careful planning, the right legal representation, and a focus on your well-being and long-term goals, it is possible to emerge from this ordeal with your rights protected and your future secured. The legal process is just one phase of your journey toward healing and a brighter tomorrow.

Remember that you are not alone—there is support available, both in the form of legal professionals who specialize in these cases and a network of friends and family who care about your well-being. While the road ahead may be filled with twists and turns, each step brings you closer to a life free from the toxic grip of a narcissistic relationship.

Through determination, resilience, and the support of those who stand by you, you can navigate the legal process with strength and grace. Ultimately, your newfound freedom and the opportunity for a healthier, happier future are well worth the effort and sacrifice required during this challenging time.

Chapter 5: Co-parenting with a narcissist:

Navigating the intricacies of co-parenting is a challenge in any divorce or separation, but when one parent exhibits narcissistic traits or has been diagnosed with NPD, the complexities can escalate to new heights. Co-parenting with a narcissist often brings a unique set of hurdles, as these individuals may prioritize their own needs and desires over the children's best interests. This section delves into the intricate and emotionally charged world of co-parenting with a narcissist. We explore the strategies, coping mechanisms, and legal considerations necessary to protect the well-being of the children involved and maintain your own sanity in the process.

Here, you'll find insights into recognizing narcissistic behavior patterns in co-parenting situations, understanding the impact on children, and strategies for establishing effective communication. We'll discuss the importance of setting boundaries and utilizing legal resources when necessary to ensure the children's needs remain at the forefront. Whether you are in the early stages of co-parenting with a narcissist or have been navigating this challenging terrain for some time, this section offers guidance and support to help you create a healthier and more stable co-parenting dynamic while safeguarding your children's emotional and psychological welfare.

Meet **Gemma and Ryan**, who find themselves entangled in the complexities of co-parenting with a narcissistic twist. Gemma, a successful professional with a commanding presence at work and home, brings her high income and assertive demeanor to the table. On the other side of this tumultuous equation is Ryan, who has taken on the role of the primary caregiver for their twin six-year-old girls.

Power struggles and relentless competition mark the dynamics between Gemma and Ryan. Gemma, driven by her narcissistic tendencies, has made her intentions abundantly clear—she will stop at nothing to gain the upper hand in their co-parenting arrangement, including engaging in a contentious custody battle that she knows will inflict emotional distress on Ryan.

As Gemma and Ryan embark on this challenging co-parenting journey, they must navigate not only the typical challenges that arise in such situations but also the added layers of narcissism and high-stakes power plays. The well-being of their twin daughters hangs in the balance as they grapple with the intricacies of co-parenting, legal battles, and the emotional toll it takes on their lives. This scenario serves as a poignant backdrop for exploring the complexities of co-parenting with a narcissist and the strategies and considerations essential for safeguarding the children's best interests in the midst of such challenging circumstances.

Protecting children from the conflict

Maintaining boundaries and shielding children from conflict are paramount when co-parenting with a narcissist. Here are some general strategies to help parents in such challenging situations:

1. **Establish Clear Communication Boundaries:** Limit communication with the narcissistic co-parent to essential matters related to the children. Use written communication like email or text messages to maintain a record of interactions, which can be valuable in legal proceedings.

2. **Parallel Parenting:** Parallel parenting can be more effective than co-parenting in high-conflict situations. This approach minimizes direct contact between parents and focuses on separate parenting responsibilities. Each parent makes decisions during their custody time without interference from the other.

3. **Use a Parenting Plan:** Develop a comprehensive parenting plan that outlines custody arrangements, visitation schedules, and decision-making responsibilities. Having a well-documented plan reduces the need for constant negotiations and minimizes conflicts.

4. **Utilize Parenting Apps:** Consider using co-parenting apps or online tools designed to facilitate communication and shared parenting responsibilities. These apps can help maintain a structured and organized approach to co-parenting.

5. **Seek Professional Support:** Consult a family therapist or counselor specializing in high-conflict divorces and co-parenting with narcissists. Professional guidance can help you navigate the emotional challenges and develop strategies to protect your children.

6. **Educate Yourself:** Learn about narcissistic behaviors and manipulation tactics so you can recognize when they are being used. Understanding the dynamics can help you respond effectively and protect your children.

7. **Stay Consistent:** Maintain consistency in parenting approaches and routines in both households. Children benefit

from predictability and stability, which can counterbalance the instability caused by a narcissistic co-parent.

8. **Empower Your Children:** Teach your children age-appropriate coping strategies and communication skills. Encourage them to express their feelings and concerns, and assure them they are not responsible for the conflict between their parents.

9. **Consider Supervised Visitation:** If necessary, explore supervised visitation options to ensure the safety and well-being of your children during interactions with the narcissistic co-parent. This can be especially crucial if there are concerns about manipulation or emotional abuse.

10. **Document and Record:** Record any incidents, interactions, or concerns related to the narcissistic co-parent. Document instances of behavior that may harm the children, as this information may be valuable in legal proceedings.

11. **Engage Legal Counsel:** Consult with an experienced family law lawyer who understands the complexities of co-parenting with a narcissist. Legal guidance is essential for protecting your rights and advocating for your children's best interests.

12. **Utilize Court Orders:** If the narcissistic co-parent violates court orders or engages in behavior that endangers the children, promptly report the violations to your lawyer and the court. Seek enforcement of court orders to ensure compliance.

13. **Self-Care:** Prioritize self-care to manage the stress and emotional toll of co-parenting with a narcissist. Maintaining

your own well-being enables you to be a more stable and supportive parent for your children.

While co-parenting with a narcissist is undeniably challenging, these strategies can help you establish boundaries and protect your children from the damaging effects of conflict. Your commitment to providing a stable and loving environment for your children can mitigate the negative impact of a narcissistic co-parent and contribute to their emotional resilience and well-being.

For Ryan, there are a few things that he can focus on when co-parenting with Gemma:

1. **Maintain Strict Boundaries:** Given Gemma's narcissistic tendencies and inclination toward power plays, Ryan must establish and maintain clear boundaries. This means limiting communication with Gemma to matters directly related to their twin daughters and avoiding any engagement in personal or contentious discussions. Ryan should use written communication, such as email or text messages, to ensure that all exchanges are documented and can serve as evidence if needed. By setting strict boundaries, Ryan can reduce opportunities for conflict and manipulation.

2. **Implement Parallel Parenting:** In high-conflict situations like this, parallel parenting is often more practical than traditional co-parenting. Ryan and Gemma can minimize direct interaction by focusing on their separate parenting responsibilities during their custody times. This approach allows Ryan to make decisions regarding their daughters' well-being

without Gemma's interference, reducing the potential for power struggles and conflicts over parenting choices.

3. **Engage a Professional Mediator or Therapist:** Given the complex dynamics at play and the narcissistic traits exhibited by Gemma, it may be beneficial for Ryan to involve a professional mediator or family therapist with experience in high-conflict co-parenting situations. A neutral third party can facilitate communication between Ryan and Gemma, ensuring that discussions remain child-focused and productive. Additionally, a therapist can guide and support both parents in managing the emotional challenges of co-parenting with a narcissist and help them find common ground when making decisions about their daughters.

By maintaining boundaries, implementing parallel parenting, and seeking professional assistance when needed, Ryan can create a more stable and less conflict-ridden co-parenting dynamic that ultimately benefits the children.

Good Communication is Critical

Effective communication is a cornerstone of successful co-parenting, especially in high-conflict situations where narcissistic behaviors may be present. Here's a general discussion of the importance of effective communication in co-parenting with a narcissist:

Communicating in writing offers several advantages. It allows for ***clarity in conveying information and expectations***. With written communication, there's a record of all interactions, which can be invaluable if disputes arise or for legal purposes. It ensures that both parents have a clear understanding of the information exchanged.

When communicating with a narcissistic co-parent, it's essential to keep messages **concise and focused** on the matter at hand—usually child-related issues. Avoid getting drawn into personal attacks, emotional exchanges, or irrelevant topics. Narcissists may use emotional manipulation, so staying on-topic helps maintain boundaries.

Engaging in personal attacks or responding to provocations from a narcissistic co-parent can escalate conflicts and create a toxic co-parenting environment. Instead, **focus on the facts and child-related concerns**, avoiding inflammatory language or emotional responses. Stick to the high road, even when provoked.

Pausing and collecting your thoughts before responding is crucial when dealing with a narcissistic co-parent. Narcissists may use tactics to trigger emotional reactions. You can avoid falling into their manipulation traps and maintain your emotional composure by pausing and responding thoughtfully.

Narcissistic co-parents often thrive on drama and conflict. You take away their power by refusing to engage in their attempts to create chaos or draw you into disputes. **Rising above the drama** means remaining calm, composed, and focused on the children's best interests, not reacting to provocations, and not feeding into their need for attention.

Demonstrating effective communication and conflict resolution skills sets a *positive example for your children*. They can learn how to navigate difficult situations and relationships healthily and constructively from your behavior.

In some cases, using a *neutral third party*, such as a mediator or co-parenting app, can facilitate communication. These resources can help keep discussions child-focused, minimize emotional confrontations, and ensure that information is exchanged efficiently.

When necessary, consult with your lawyer before responding to any communication that may have *legal implications*. Legal professionals can provide guidance on how to protect your rights and make informed decisions.

Effective communication is essential for co-parenting success, especially when dealing with a narcissistic co-parent. By prioritizing clarity, staying focused on child-related matters, avoiding personal attacks, pausing before responding, and rising above drama and manipulation, you can create a healthier co-parenting dynamic that safeguards the well-being of your children while minimizing conflict.

Ryan can focus on these things when communicating with Gemma in their co-parenting dynamic:

1. **Maintain a Child-Centered Approach:** When communicating with Gemma, always focus on their twin daughters' well-being and best interests. Frame your messages around their needs, schedules, and any important developments in their lives. By consistently demonstrating your commitment to their welfare, you can minimize potential conflicts during discussions.

2. **Stick to the Facts and Be Concise:** Given Gemma's narcissistic tendencies, Ryan needs to keep messages factual, concise, and devoid of personal attacks or emotional content. Stick to the relevant information or requests, avoiding unnecessary details or emotive language. Narcissists often use emotional manipulation, so maintaining a fact-based communication style helps maintain boundaries.

3. **Set Boundaries and Utilize a Third Party:** Establish and assert clear boundaries in your communication with Gemma. If Ryan notices that she frequently engages in manipulative or contentious behavior, he can consider involving a neutral third party, such as a mediator or co-parenting app. This external resource can help facilitate communication, ensuring that discussions remain child-focused and that important matters can be addressed without unnecessary conflict.

By staying child-centered, maintaining a fact-based approach, and setting boundaries, Ryan can contribute to a more stable co-parenting dynamic while prioritizing the well-being of their twin daughters and minimizing the potential for conflicts and emotional manipulation.

Document everything

Documenting everything is essential in the context of co-parenting with a narcissist for several important reasons.

Clear and comprehensive ***documentation can be vital*** evidence in legal proceedings. If disputes escalate to court, having a record of interactions, agreements, and incidents can substantiate your claims and protect your rights as a parent.

Memory can be unreliable, especially in emotionally charged situations. Documentation ensures an ***accurate and objective record*** of past events and conversations. This can help you recall details and provide a factual account of what transpired.

Documenting your attempts to communicate and collaborate with the narcissistic co-parent demonstrates your commitment to a healthy co-parenting relationship. These documents can show your willingness to cooperate and your efforts to prioritize the children's well-being. Written communication, such as emails and text messages, can provide a clear and objective record of interactions. This documentation can demonstrate your attempts to communicate effectively and address essential matters related to the children.

Narcissistic co-parents may engage in manipulative or harmful behavior. Documenting such behavior ***creates a track record*** that can be helpful in legal proceedings or when seeking intervention from professionals, such as therapists or mediators. Over time, documentation can reveal patterns of behavior or tactics the narcissistic co-parent uses. Recognizing these patterns can help you anticipate and respond to their actions more effectively.

Keeping records of decisions made jointly with the co-parent, especially those related to the children's education, health, and extracurricular activities, can help prevent disputes and ensure everyone is on the same page. When working with therapists, mediators, or other professionals involved in the co-parenting process, having a documented history of interactions and concerns can provide valuable context and support your case.

Documentation can help **ensure both parties adhere to court orders and custody agreements**. If there are violations, such records can be used to seek legal remedies.

Knowing you have a thorough record of your co-parenting efforts can provide **peace of mind**. It lets you focus on the children's well-being rather than constantly worrying about disputes or misunderstandings.

Documenting everything is a proactive and protective measure when co-parenting with a narcissist. It provides a factual record of interactions, behavior patterns, and decisions, which can be invaluable for legal purposes, maintaining accountability, and safeguarding the children's best interests.

Protecting your children from the dispute

Focusing on the children's well-being, shielding them from adverse effects, and maintaining a focus on positive parenting is critical for several compelling reasons:

Children exposed to conflict, manipulation, or emotional distress between their parents can suffer significant emotional and psychological harm. **Protecting children's emotional health** and prioritizing their well-being helps protect them from unnecessary stress and emotional trauma.

Children thrive on ***stability and routine***. Positive parenting practices ensure children have a consistent and predictable environment, which is essential for their emotional development and overall sense of security.

Parents serve as role models for children. Parents can teach their children valuable life skills, including conflict resolution, empathy, and resilience, by ***demonstrating positive parenting behaviors***, even in challenging circumstances.

Shielding children from the negative effects of parental conflict and narcissistic behaviors can ***mitigate the potential long-term impact on their mental health*** and relationships. Providing a safe and supportive environment can help children develop healthy coping mechanisms.

Encouraging a focus on the children's well-being ***promotes a cooperative and child-centered approach*** to co-parenting. This, in turn, can lead to healthier and more stable relationships between the parents, which can benefit the children.

Courts prioritize the children's best interests when deciding parenting arrangements. Demonstrating a commitment to positive parenting and the children's well-being can strengthen your case in legal proceedings.

Shielding children from negative dynamics ***empowers them to form their own opinions*** and make informed decisions about their relationships with each parent. It allows them to maintain a sense of agency and autonomy.

Home should be a safe haven for children, where they can feel loved, supported, and free from the stress of parental conflicts. Positive parenting practices contribute to the creation of this safe and nurturing environment.

Encouraging resilience in children means equipping them with the tools to overcome adversity. Positive parenting fosters resilience by teaching children how to navigate challenges and cope with difficult situations.

Focusing on the children's well-being and positive parenting practices ***contribute to their healthy development***. They are more likely to grow up emotionally secure, confident, and capable of forming healthy relationships.

These principles become even more crucial in co-parenting situations involving a narcissistic ex-partner. By consistently prioritizing the children's well-being, shielding them from negative influences, and focusing on positive parenting, parents can help their children navigate the challenges posed by a narcissistic co-parent and ensure their overall growth and happiness.

Navigating co-parenting with a relentless narcissistic co-parent like Gemma can be exceptionally challenging, but Ryan can employ several strategies to shield their twin daughters from her attacks and maintain a focus on positive parenting:

1. **Gray Rock Method:** The Gray Rock Method involves becoming emotionally unresponsive to the narcissistic co-parent's provocations. Ryan can keep his interactions with Gemma emotionally neutral, avoiding emotional reactions or

engaging in arguments. By doing so, he makes himself less of a target for her attacks.

2. **Use Written Communication:** Communicating in writing, such as through emails or text messages, provides a record of interactions and allows Ryan to maintain a fact-based, child-focused approach. It also reduces the opportunity for heated verbal exchanges.

3. **Consult with Professionals:** Enlisting the help of professionals, such as therapists or mediators, can provide a structured and neutral environment for communication. These experts can guide discussions and help keep them child-centered, minimizing the impact of Gemma's attacks.

4. **Seek Legal Protection:** If Gemma's relentless attacks escalate to harassment or threats, Ryan should consult with his lawyer to explore legal avenues for protection, such as restraining orders or modifications to the custody agreement.

5. **Keep Detailed Records:** Ryan should maintain thorough records of all interactions with Gemma, including dates, times, and communication content. This documentation can be valuable if legal action is necessary or if he needs to demonstrate a pattern of behavior.

6. **Focus on Consistency:** Ryan can provide their twin daughters with a consistent and stable environment. Maintaining routines and predictability can help shield them from the emotional turbulence created by Gemma's attacks.

7. **Involve the Children's School:** Communicating with the school and teachers can help ensure the children's educational environment remains supportive and nurturing. School staff can also serve as additional sources of emotional support for the children.

8. **Emphasize Healthy Coping Mechanisms:** Teach the children healthy ways to cope with stress and conflict. Encourage open communication, allowing them to express their feelings and concerns.

9. **Utilize Support Systems:** Lean on the support of friends and family who can provide emotional support and assistance with childcare when needed. These support systems can help alleviate some of the stress caused by Gemma's attacks.

10. **Self-Care:** Ryan must prioritize self-care to maintain his own emotional and mental well-being. By caring for himself, he can better support the children and provide a stable and nurturing environment.

In the face of relentless attacks from Gemma, Ryan must maintain his composure, prioritize the children's well-being, and seek professional and legal support when necessary. While challenging, these strategies can help shield the children from the negative impact of Gemma's behavior and create a healthier co-parenting dynamic.

Navigating co-parenting with a narcissistic ex-partner, as demonstrated in the challenging dynamic between Gemma and Ryan, is undeniably tricky. However, it is not an impossible task. Throughout this section, we've explored strategies and principles to help parents shield their children from the adverse effects of a narcissistic co-parent while focusing on positive parenting.

It is crucial to remember that the well-being of the children must remain the top priority. Parents like Ryan can counterbalance the turmoil created by a relentless narcissistic co-parent by consistently providing a stable and nurturing environment, emphasizing routines, and promoting open communication.

Additionally, seeking professional support, maintaining detailed records, and knowing when to engage in legal protection are essential steps in preserving the children's well-being and the parent's own emotional health.

Co-parenting with a narcissist is a journey fraught with challenges, but by employing these strategies and staying committed to the children's best interests, parents can create a nurturing and loving environment that fosters the children's growth and happiness.

Moving forward, we will delve deeper into the healing and recovery process, focusing on parents and children. Recovery is a crucial step toward rebuilding after the turmoil of a narcissistic relationship and co-parenting dynamic. In the next section, we will explore the journey toward healing, resilience, and, ultimately, finding a path to a brighter future for all involved.

Chapter 6: Recovery and Healing

Recovery and healing are profoundly transformative processes that follow periods of adversity, trauma, or challenging life experiences. These journeys encompass emotional, psychological, and sometimes physical restoration, ultimately leading individuals toward a renewed sense of well-being and wholeness. Recovery signifies a path toward reclaiming one's life, finding strength within vulnerability, and rediscovering a sense of purpose and joy. On the other hand, healing represents a profound process of self-repair and growth, transcending past wounds to create a brighter and more fulfilling future. Both recovery and healing are unique to each individual, shaped by their experiences, resilience, and the support systems they engage. These processes are marked by self-compassion, self-discovery, and the gradual emergence of inner strength, offering a path towards greater inner peace, personal growth, and a renewed connection with the world.

As we work through the important stages of recovery and healing, let's meet **Josie and Mike**.

Josie and Mike met in their mid-20s through mutual friends and quickly fell in love. On the surface, their relationship appeared idyllic, filled with passion, adventure, and shared interests. Josie was charming, charismatic, and captivating, drawing Mike into her world with her magnetic personality.

However, beneath the surface, their relationship was marked by tumultuous dynamics. Josie exhibited classic signs of narcissism, constantly seeking admiration and validation. She craved attention from Mike and expected him to prioritize her needs and desires above all else. This self-absorption often left Mike feeling neglected and unheard.

As the relationship progressed, Josie's behavior became increasingly manipulative. She would gaslight Mike, making him doubt his own perceptions and feelings. When Mike attempted to express his concerns or emotions, Josie would dismiss him, belittle his feelings, or shift the blame onto him. Mike's self-esteem eroded over time, and he began to doubt his own worth.

Josie's need for control extended beyond emotional manipulation. She would dictate Mike's social interactions, isolating him from friends and family. She insisted on making significant decisions for both of them, leaving Mike feeling powerless and trapped.

Their relationship was marked by constant turmoil, with frequent arguments and emotional outbursts from Josie. Despite the mounting challenges, Mike remained dedicated to the relationship, hoping to salvage what was once a passionate connection.

Mike's mental and emotional well-being suffered as time passed, and he felt trapped in a never-ending cycle of Josie's narcissistic behaviors.

The importance of self-care during and after divorce

Self-care during and after divorce holds paramount importance, and this significance is magnified when you have been in a relationship with a narcissist. Divorce is a challenging life transition that can take an emotional and physical toll on anyone, but when coupled with the unique dynamics of narcissistic abuse, self-care becomes not just important but crucial for recovery and healing.

Narcissistic relationships often erode one's sense of self, leaving individuals feeling diminished and worthless. Self-care allows you to **rediscover and reconnect with your true self**. It's an act of asserting your identity and nurturing your self-worth, helping you break free from the narcissist's devaluation.

Narcissists thrive on tearing down their partners' self-esteem. Whether practicing mindfulness, seeking therapy, or pursuing hobbies, engaging in self-care activities can help **rebuild your self-esteem and self-confidence**. These practices remind you that you are worthy of love and respect.

Divorce from a narcissist often leaves emotional scars. **Self-care provides a safe space to process these emotions**, whether through journaling, therapy, or support groups. It allows you to grieve the loss of the relationship, release pent-up emotions, and gradually find emotional healing.

Narcissistic abuse can take a toll on your physical health. Neglecting self-care can exacerbate stress-related health issues. **Prioritizing physical self-care**, such as exercise, a balanced diet, and adequate sleep, can help restore your vitality and resilience.

Narcissists are notorious for violating boundaries. Self-care helps you **establish and maintain healthy boundaries**, teaching you to protect your well-being from further harm. It reinforces the importance of self-preservation and signals that your needs matter.

Divorce is inherently stressful. Engaging in self-care practices, like meditation, deep breathing exercises, or relaxation techniques, can mitigate stress, promote emotional stability, and **enhance your ability to cope** with challenges.

Narcissistic relationships can be joy-sapping. Self-care activities that **bring joy and pleasure back into your life** are essential. Whether it's rediscovering hobbies or exploring new interests, these moments of happiness reinforce that life can be fulfilling and enjoyable.

Narcissistic abuse is a traumatic experience. Self-care facilitates post-traumatic growth, allowing you to **emerge stronger, wiser, and more resilient** from the ordeal. It becomes a path towards rebuilding your life on healthier foundations.

By practicing self-care and healing from the scars of narcissistic abuse, you become **better equipped to enter future relationships** from a position of strength and self-assuredness. It reduces the likelihood of falling into similar abusive dynamics.

Self-care is a lifeline during and after divorce, particularly when recovering from a relationship with a narcissist. It is a multi-faceted approach to healing that addresses emotional, psychological, and physical well-being. By engaging in self-care practices, you reclaim your sense of self and take significant steps toward a brighter, more empowered, and abuse-free future. It is a powerful tool that allows you to not just survive but thrive beyond the challenges of divorce and narcissistic abuse.

Dealing with trauma and rebuilding self-esteem

Understanding trauma is profoundly relevant to healing from a narcissistic relationship. In such relationships, individuals often endure emotional, psychological, and sometimes even physical abuse, leaving them with deep emotional scars. Recognizing the traumatic nature of the experience is the first step in the healing process. It validates the pain and suffering endured and helps individuals realize that their reactions, such as anxiety, depression, or PTSD, are normal responses to trauma.

Remember the warning in the introduction for this book – it's relevant here. **Do not try to use this information to self-diagnose or treat**. This is information only. If you find yourself in a relationship with a person who has narcissistic traits or NPD seek professional assistance from a qualified therapist to help you.

Rebuilding self-esteem after a narcissistic relationship is a complex yet crucial endeavor. Trauma from the relationship can shatter one's self-worth, as narcissists consistently devalue and undermine their partners.

To rebuild self-esteem, individuals must:

1. **Self-Reflection:** Reflect on the relationship and acknowledge the abuse endured. Understanding how narcissistic manipulation works can help individuals depersonalize the abuse and realize it does not reflect their worth.

2. **Seek Professional Help:** Trauma therapy or counseling with a therapist experienced in narcissistic abuse recovery can be

immensely beneficial. Therapy provides a safe space to process the trauma, identify its impact, and develop coping strategies.

3. **Self-Compassion:** Practice self-compassion by treating oneself with the same kindness and understanding that one would offer to a friend in a similar situation. This must include challenging self-blame and self-criticism.

4. **Setting Boundaries:** Learning to establish and enforce healthy boundaries is essential. It prevents further abuse and reinforces a sense of self-worth. Boundaries protect emotional well-being and foster self-respect.

5. **Reconnecting with Interests:** Reengage in activities and hobbies that once brought joy and fulfillment. This helps individuals rediscover their passions, reminding them of their unique qualities and talents.

6. **Support System:** Surround oneself with a supportive network of friends and family who understand the trauma experienced and offer encouragement. Seek out support groups or communities of survivors who share similar experiences.

7. **Positive Affirmations:** Replace negative self-talk with positive affirmations. Remind oneself of strengths, accomplishments, and qualities that make you valuable and unique.

8. **Mindfulness and Self-Care:** Practice mindfulness and self-care regularly. This involves staying present in the moment, managing stress, and nurturing physical and emotional well-

being through activities such as meditation, exercise, and relaxation techniques.

9. **Forgiveness:** Not for the narcissist's benefit but for your own, consider forgiveness. Forgiveness is a process of letting go of the anger and resentment that can consume you after trauma. It doesn't mean condoning the abuse but liberating yourself from its emotional grip.

10. **Rebuilding Trust:** Trusting oneself and others again is crucial to self-esteem recovery. It's a gradual process that may involve therapy to address trust issues stemming from the narcissistic relationship.

Understanding the trauma inherent in a narcissistic relationship is the first step towards healing and rebuilding self-esteem. It acknowledges the pain endured and validates one's emotional responses. Rebuilding self-esteem is a multi-faceted journey that involves self-reflection, professional help, self-compassion, boundary setting, rediscovering interests, building a support system, positive affirmations, mindfulness, self-care, forgiveness, and rebuilding trust. It is a process of self-discovery and self-empowerment, ultimately leading to a healthier and more resilient sense of self.

Let's return to Mike and Josie's relationship. Mike has ended the relationship with Josie. He feels pretty low and deals with many emotions he doesn't understand. Mike used to be such a confident guy – why can't he go back to feeling like that? Mike feels stuck, like this is all his fault.

Dealing with the trauma caused by a relationship with a narcissistic partner like Josie can be challenging but essential for someone like Mike. Here are some steps Mike can take to navigate his healing journey:

1. **Recognize and Accept the Trauma:** The first step is acknowledging that the relationship with Josie was traumatic. Mike should understand that it's normal to experience emotional scars after such an experience and that his feelings are valid.

2. **Seek Professional Help:** Trauma therapy or counseling with a therapist experienced in narcissistic abuse recovery can be invaluable. A qualified therapist can help Mike process his emotions, identify the impact of the abuse, and develop coping strategies to manage trauma-related symptoms. Mike should learn about narcissistic personality disorder and the tactics narcissists use. It can help Mike recognize the abusive behaviors he endured and depersonalize them, understanding that they were not a reflection of his worth.

3. **Establish Boundaries:** Learning to set and enforce healthy boundaries is crucial for healing. Mike should practice saying no and assertively protecting his well-being from further harm. This includes minimizing contact with Josie if possible. Mike should also identify and reduce exposure to triggers that evoke painful memories or emotions related to his time with Josie. This may include avoiding places or situations associated with the trauma.

4. **Self-Compassion & Self-Care:** Mike should practice self-compassion by treating himself with kindness and understanding. Challenging self-blame and self-criticism is important, recognizing that he was a victim of manipulation and abuse. Further, regular self-care is essential for healing. Mike should prioritize physical and emotional well-being through exercise, mindfulness, relaxation techniques, and hobbies that bring joy and fulfillment.

5. **Support System:** Surrounding himself with a supportive network of friends and family who understand the trauma experienced can provide emotional bolstering. Support groups or communities of survivors can offer shared experiences and validation.

Healing from the trauma caused by a narcissistic relationship takes time and patience. Mike should remember that his journey is unique, and progress may be nonlinear. By seeking professional help, practicing self-compassion, establishing boundaries, and engaging in self-care, he can gradually reclaim his sense of self and move toward a healthier and more fulfilling life.

Therapeutic approaches for healing from narcissistic abuse

Healing from narcissistic abuse often requires specialized therapeutic approaches, and seeking a therapist or counselor with expertise in this area is crucial for several reasons:

1. **Specialized Knowledge**: Narcissistic abuse is a complex and unique form of emotional and psychological abuse. Specialists in narcissistic abuse understand the intricacies of narcissistic personality disorder and the tactics they use to manipulate and control their victims. This knowledge allows them to tailor therapeutic techniques to address the nuances of such abuse.

2. **Validation and Understanding:** A specialized therapist or counselor can provide validation and understanding that may be lacking elsewhere. They recognize the profound impact narcissistic abuse has on victims' mental and emotional well-being and can validate the trauma experienced.

3. **Safe Space:** Victims of narcissistic abuse often feel isolated and unheard. A specialist therapist creates a safe and non-judgmental space where survivors can openly discuss their experiences without fear of blame or disbelief.

4. **Tailored Approaches:** Specialized therapists employ evidence-based therapeutic approaches designed to address narcissistic abuse's aftermath. These approaches may include trauma-focused therapies, cognitive-behavioral therapy (CBT), dialectical behavior therapy (DBT), and schema therapy, among others.

5. **Coping Strategies:** Narcissistic abuse can lead to a range of emotional and psychological symptoms, including anxiety, depression, PTSD, and low self-esteem. A specialist therapist can teach survivors coping strategies to manage these symptoms effectively.

6. **Boundary Setting:** Setting and maintaining healthy boundaries is crucial to recovery from narcissistic abuse. Specialized therapists help survivors develop assertiveness skills and boundary-setting techniques to protect themselves from further harm.

7. **Emotional Processing:** Victims of narcissistic abuse often have unresolved emotions and trauma. Specialized therapists guide survivors through emotionally processing the abuse, allowing them to release pent-up feelings and regain emotional stability.

8. **Rebuilding Self-Esteem:** Rebuilding self-esteem after narcissistic abuse is a delicate process. Therapists with expertise in this area can help survivors recognize their worth, challenge negative self-beliefs, and foster self-compassion.

9. **Post-Traumatic Growth:** A specialized therapist can assist survivors in harnessing the potential for post-traumatic growth, helping them emerge from the trauma with greater resilience, wisdom, and personal growth.

10. **Support and Validation:** Survivors of narcissistic abuse often benefit from validation and support from others who understand their experiences. Therapeutic groups or support communities facilitated by specialists can provide this crucial support network.

Healing from narcissistic abuse is a complex and sensitive journey requiring specialized therapeutic approaches. Seeking a therapist or counselor with expertise in narcissistic abuse is essential to receive the validation, understanding, and tailored support needed to navigate the healing process effectively. It ensures that survivors receive the specific tools and techniques required to address the unique challenges of narcissistic abuse and empowers them to regain control over their lives and well-being.

Understanding complex post-traumatic stress disorder

Complex Post-Traumatic Stress Disorder (C-PTSD) is a psychological condition that can develop in individuals exposed to prolonged and repeated traumatic events, typically involving interpersonal abuse, neglect, or exploitation. Unlike traditional Post-Traumatic Stress Disorder (PTSD), which is often associated with a single traumatic incident, C-PTSD is characterized by a pattern of chronic and ongoing trauma.

Remember – this is information only and you should ***see a qualified therapist if you are worried about your mental health*** following your relationship.

Key features of C-PTSD include:

1. **Exposure to Prolonged Trauma:** C-PTSD is typically associated with exposure to traumatic events that occur over an extended period, such as childhood abuse, domestic violence, human trafficking, or captivity. These experiences often involve a power imbalance and repeated victimization.

2. **Complex Symptoms:** C-PTSD involves a range of emotional, psychological, and physical symptoms that can be more pervasive and enduring than those seen in traditional PTSD. Symptoms often include flashbacks, nightmares, emotional dysregulation, dissociation, and severe anxiety.

3. **Identity and Self-Concept:** Individuals with C-PTSD may struggle with a distorted self-concept and difficulty forming a coherent identity. The prolonged exposure to trauma can lead to feelings of shame, guilt, and a diminished sense of self-worth.

4. **Emotional Dysregulation:** Emotional regulation is often impaired in individuals with C-PTSD. They may experience intense mood swings, anger, irritability, and difficulty managing emotional reactions.

5. **Relationship Difficulties:** C-PTSD can challenge forming and maintaining healthy relationships. Trust issues, fear of abandonment, and difficulties with attachment are common.

6. **Somatic Symptoms:** Physical symptoms, such as chronic pain, gastrointestinal problems, and other somatic complaints, are frequently associated with C-PTSD. These symptoms can be a manifestation of the emotional distress and physiological changes resulting from prolonged trauma.

7. **Hypervigilance:** Individuals with C-PTSD often exhibit hypervigilance, heightened alertness, and constant scanning for potential threats. This survival response can persist even after the traumatic events have ended.

8. **Dissociation:** Dissociation involves a disconnection from one's thoughts, identity, consciousness, or memory. It can be a coping mechanism in response to overwhelming trauma and can manifest as periods of feeling disconnected from reality.

9. **Impact on Functioning:** C-PTSD can significantly impair a person's daily functioning, affecting their ability to work, engage in relationships, and enjoy life. Substance abuse and self-destructive behaviors may also be present as maladaptive coping mechanisms.

It's important to note that C-PTSD is not officially recognized in all diagnostic manuals like the DSM-5. However, it is widely discussed and understood within the mental health community as a distinct and severe form of post-traumatic stress disorder that results from chronic and complex trauma.

Treatment for C-PTSD typically involves a combination of therapies, including trauma-focused therapy, cognitive-behavioral therapy (CBT), dialectical behavior therapy (DBT), and other approaches tailored to address the specific symptoms and challenges associated with complex trauma. Treatment aims to help individuals heal from their past experiences, manage symptoms, and improve their overall well-being and quality of life.

Not everyone in a relationship with a narcissist will develop Post-Traumatic Stress Disorder (PTSD). While narcissistic abuse can be highly distressing and traumatic, the development of PTSD is influenced by a combination of factors, including the individual's resilience, coping mechanisms, and the severity and duration of the abuse.

Here are some key points to consider:

1. **Vulnerability:** Individuals vary in their vulnerability to developing PTSD. Some people may have pre-existing factors, such as a history of trauma or mental health conditions, that make them more susceptible to developing PTSD in response to narcissistic abuse.

2. **Severity of Abuse:** The severity and intensity of the narcissistic abuse can impact the likelihood of developing PTSD. Prolonged and severe abuse is more likely to result in traumatic stress symptoms.

3. **Coping Mechanisms:** How individuals cope with the abuse plays a significant role. Some people may have healthier coping mechanisms, social support networks, or access to therapy that can mitigate the development of PTSD symptoms.

4. **Resilience:** Resilience, or the ability to bounce back from adversity, can also influence whether someone develops PTSD. Some individuals may have greater resilience and psychological resources to manage the emotional impact of the abuse.

5. **Timely Intervention:** Early intervention and support can be crucial in preventing the development of PTSD. Seeking therapy and support as soon as possible can help individuals process their experiences and develop effective coping strategies.

6. **Complexity of Trauma:** Narcissistic abuse can be complex and varied. Not all narcissistic relationships are the same, and the trauma experienced can range from emotional manipulation

to physical abuse. The complexity of the trauma can affect the development of PTSD.

It's important to note that while not everyone in a relationship with a narcissist will develop PTSD, many individuals may still experience emotional and psychological distress, such as anxiety, depression, low self-esteem, and other trauma-related symptoms. ***Seeking therapy and support is essential*** for those who have been in narcissistic relationships to address these emotional challenges and work towards healing and recovery, whether or not they meet the criteria for a formal PTSD diagnosis.

Embracing forgiveness and letting go of resentment

Embracing forgiveness and letting go of resentment is a critical component of recovery and healing, particularly after experiencing narcissistic abuse. Forgiveness in this context does not mean condoning or excusing the abuser's actions; instead, it is a deeply personal process that primarily benefits the survivor.

Firstly, ***forgiveness frees the survivor from the heavy burden*** of carrying anger, bitterness, and resentment. Holding onto these negative emotions can perpetuate the emotional wounds inflicted by the narcissistic relationship, keeping the survivor trapped in a cycle of pain and suffering. Letting go allows room for healing, inner peace, and emotional relief.

Secondly, forgiveness ***empowers survivors*** to reclaim control over their lives and well-being. By forgiving the abuser, survivors shift the focus from the perpetrator's actions to their own healing and growth.

It is a declaration of resilience and a commitment to moving forward rather than dwelling on the past.

Moreover, forgiveness can **break the cycle of victimhood**. Survivors of narcissistic abuse often feel powerless and victimized. Choosing to forgive is an act of self-empowerment, signifying that the survivor is no longer defined by the abuse but by their ability to transcend it.

Additionally, letting go of resentment *facilitates emotional healing and recovery*. It creates space for positive emotions, self-compassion, and self-love to flourish. This, in turn, can improve self-esteem and self-worth, which are often deeply impacted by narcissistic abuse.

Forgiveness also **supports the survivor's mental and physical health**. Chronic anger and resentment can contribute to stress-related health issues, such as high blood pressure and anxiety. Letting go of these emotions promotes overall well-being and reduces the risk of ongoing health problems.

Lastly, forgiveness does not imply reconciliation with the abuser or forgetting the past. It means **releasing the emotional grip that the abuser has on the survivor's life**. It acknowledges that the survivor deserves peace and happiness beyond the shadow of the narcissistic relationship.

Embracing forgiveness and letting go of resentment is vital to recovery and healing from narcissistic abuse. It allows survivors to reclaim control, break free from the cycle of victimization, promote emotional well-being, and ultimately, build a brighter and more fulfilling future.

Someone like Mike, who has experienced narcissistic abuse in a relationship with someone like Josie, can benefit significantly from embracing forgiveness and letting go of resentment in several ways.

Letting go of resentment *frees Mike from the emotional burden* he may have been carrying since the abusive relationship. He can experience a profound sense of relief as he releases the anger and bitterness associated with the past, allowing him to breathe more freely and feel lighter emotionally.

Forgiveness is a pivotal step in **healing and recovery**. It signifies that the trauma inflicted by Josie no longer defines Mike. By choosing forgiveness, he shifts his focus toward his own well-being and growth, promoting emotional healing and resilience.

Forgiveness is an act of **personal empowerment**. It signifies that Mike is taking control of his own life and emotions. It demonstrates that he is no longer allowing Josie's actions to hold power over him. This empowerment can boost his self-esteem and self-worth.

Letting go of resentment allows Mike to **cultivate a more optimistic outlook on life**. It creates space for hope, happiness, and optimism to flourish. This shift in perspective can improve his overall mental and emotional well-being.

As Mike heals and forgives, he may find it **easier to form and maintain healthy relationships** with others. Letting go of the anger and distrust associated with the abuse can improve interpersonal connections and increase trust in others.

Forgiveness can have **positive effects on physical health**. By releasing chronic anger and resentment, Mike can reduce stress levels and lower the risk of stress-related health issues, contributing to better overall health and well-being.

Embracing forgiveness allows Mike to **focus on personal growth and self-improvement**. He can set new goals, pursue his passions, and work towards a more fulfilling life without being weighed down by the past.

Forgiveness can provide a **sense of closure and resolution** to the trauma. It signifies that Mike is ready to move forward and put the past behind him, allowing him to embrace a new chapter in his life with a sense of peace.

It's important to note that forgiveness is a deeply personal and individual process. Mike may not arrive at forgiveness quickly or easily, and that's perfectly normal. It's a journey that takes time and self-compassion. Seeking support from a therapist or counselor experienced in narcissistic abuse recovery can be invaluable in helping Mike navigate this process and reap the many benefits that forgiveness can offer in his journey toward healing and transformation.

Chapter 7: Starting Over: Building a New Life

Embarking on the journey of starting over after the tumultuous experience of co-parenting with a narcissist can be both daunting and liberating. In this section, we explore essential themes of rediscovering personal identity, setting new goals, rebuilding social connections, embracing new hobbies, and nurturing personal growth.

One of the most significant challenges individuals face after navigating a narcissistic relationship and its aftermath is regaining a sense of self and purpose. The narcissistic dynamic often involves manipulation and control, leaving individuals feeling lost, depleted, and disconnected from their identities.

However, as the dust settles, there emerges an opportunity for transformation. Reclaiming personal identity involves peeling back the layers of external influence and rediscovering the authentic self—the person that existed before the narcissistic relationship and its trials. This process of self-discovery is a vital step toward healing and personal growth.

Setting new goals and aspirations becomes the compass that guides individuals forward. It's a chance to dream anew, to identify passions and ambitions that may have been stifled during the past relationship, and to work toward a future filled with purpose and fulfillment.

Rebuilding social connections is another crucial aspect of starting over. Narcissistic relationships often isolate individuals from their support systems. Reconnecting with friends and family or forming new connections provides a vital emotional support network and reinforces a sense of belonging.

Exploring new hobbies and interests (or rediscovering a past hobby) can be a source of joy and personal growth. It allows individuals to tap into uncharted territories of creativity, curiosity, and self-expression, fostering a sense of accomplishment and vitality.

Finally, personal growth is at the heart of starting over. It involves developing resilience, self-compassion, and a deeper understanding of one's own strengths and weaknesses. This journey toward self-improvement and empowerment is a testament to the resilience of the human spirit.

As we delve into this section, we will explore these themes, offering guidance and inspiration to those embarking on the rewarding path of building a new life after the challenges of a narcissistic relationship.

Let's meet our final couple – ***Jack and Bella***.

Jack and Bella were once deeply entwined in a tumultuous relationship. Driven by his narcissistic tendencies, Jack often placed his needs and desires above all else. Bella, recognizing the toxicity of the relationship and wanting a healthier environment for their daughter Sofia, made the difficult decision to leave Jack. She took eight-year-old Sofia with her, and the parenting arrangements were settled legally.

Despite the physical separation, the emotional turmoil continues. Jack, unwilling to relinquish his need for control and attention, makes every day challenging for Bella. His relentless attempts at manipulation, guilt-tripping, and emotional outbursts create an ongoing source of stress for Bella and Sofia.

Bella is determined to shield Sofia from the adverse effects of her father's behavior and provide her with a loving and stable environment. She recognizes that the road ahead is not easy, but her commitment to her daughter's well-being remains unwavering. In the face of Jack's relentless actions, Bella is determined to find a way to navigate co-parenting, protect Sofia, and rebuild her own life.

Rediscovering personal identity and values

Rediscovering personal identity and values is a transformative journey that follows the tumultuous experience of a narcissistic relationship. This process involves peeling back the layers of external influence and reclaiming the authentic self that may have been stifled or lost. It's an essential step towards healing, self-empowerment, and creating a life aligned with one's core beliefs and aspirations.

The first phase of rediscovery begins with *self-exploration*. Individuals need to reconnect with their inner selves, often buried beneath the demands and expectations of the narcissistic relationship. This involves introspection and a willingness to confront past wounds and insecurities. It's an opportunity to reacquaint oneself with personal preferences, values, and aspirations that may have been suppressed.

Rediscovering personal identity often involves *reigniting passions and interests* that may have been dormant. This might mean revisiting hobbies, activities, or creative pursuits that once brought joy and fulfillment. These activities can rekindle a sense of purpose and reconnect individuals with the things that genuinely resonate with their authentic selves.

Re-evaluating personal values is a pivotal part of the journey. Individuals need to discern what truly matters to them, separate from the external influences of the narcissistic relationship. This may involve questioning previous beliefs and reassessing one's ethical and moral compass. Clarity on values helps guide decisions and actions in alignment with one's true self.

Rediscovery requires ***self-compassion***. Many individuals who have endured narcissistic relationships grapple with self-doubt and self-blame. Practicing self-compassion involves treating oneself with kindness, forgiving past perceived shortcomings, and recognizing that healing is gradual.

Establishing boundaries is crucial in rediscovery. It's a way of protecting the newly rediscovered self from external intrusions and manipulations. Setting and enforcing boundaries empowers individuals to prioritize their well-being and values, even in the face of potential resistance or pressure.

The process of rediscovery can be emotionally challenging, and ***seeking support is essential***. Friends, family, or professional counselors can provide guidance, empathy, and validation as individuals navigate this transformative journey. They can offer insights and encouragement during moments of doubt or difficulty.

Rediscovering personal identity and values often leads to significant life changes. It may involve reevaluating relationships, career choices, or lifestyle decisions. ***Embracing change*** can be liberating but may also be met with resistance from those resistant to the evolving self.

Staying true to newfound values and identity requires courage and determination.

Rediscovering personal identity and values is a journey of self-discovery and self-empowerment. Through this process, individuals emerge stronger, more authentic, and better equipped to create a life aligned with their true selves and core values.

As Bella embarks on her journey to rediscover the aspects of herself that may have been chiseled away during her relationship with Jack, there are several steps she can take:

1. **Self-Reflection:** Bella can begin by engaging in deep self-reflection. This involves setting aside quiet moments to contemplate her beliefs, values, and personal interests. Journaling can be a powerful tool for self-reflection, allowing her to explore her thoughts and emotions. Through this process, Bella can identify the values and passions that were overshadowed by the dynamics of her past relationship.

2. **Reconnect with Hobbies and Interests:** Bella can revisit the hobbies and interests that once brought her joy and fulfillment. Whether painting, playing a musical instrument, hiking, or any other activity she enjoyed, engaging in these pursuits can help her reconnect with her authentic self. These activities provide a sense of accomplishment and remind her of the unique qualities and interests that make her who she is.

3. **Seek Support and Exploration:** Bella can benefit from seeking support from a therapist or counselor specializing in post-narcissistic relationship recovery. Professional guidance

can help her explore her identity and values more deeply. Additionally, joining support groups or communities of individuals who have gone through similar experiences can provide validation and encouragement during the rediscovery process.

It's essential for Bella to approach this journey with patience and self-compassion. Rediscovering oneself is a gradual process, and it's okay to acknowledge that some aspects of her identity may have evolved or changed during her experiences. Embracing her authentic self, with its unique values and interests, will ultimately empower Bella to move forward with a stronger sense of self and purpose.

Setting Goals and Envisioning a Brighter Future

Setting goals and envisioning a brighter future is a transformative process that can empower individuals to move beyond the challenges of their past, especially in the aftermath of a narcissistic relationship. This journey toward personal growth and fulfillment involves several key components:

The first step in setting goals and envisioning a brighter future is understanding what one truly desires – **being clear about your vision or the future**. Individuals must reflect on their aspirations, dreams, and passions. This process often requires digging deep to identify personal values, interests, and long-term objectives.

Individuals can begin **setting specific and achievable goals** with a clear vision. These goals may encompass various aspects of life, including career, relationships, personal development, and health.

These objectives serve as guiding stars, providing direction and purpose.

Prioritizing goals is essential, especially when dealing with the aftermath of a narcissistic relationship. It's crucial to distinguish between short-term and long-term goals and focus on what matters most. Prioritization helps individuals allocate their time, energy, and resources effectively.

Large goals can be overwhelming, but breaking them down into **smaller, manageable steps** makes them more attainable. These smaller milestones act as building blocks, allowing individuals to track progress and stay motivated.

Setting and working towards goals often involves facing setbacks and challenges. **Building emotional resilience** is vital in overcoming obstacles. This resilience enables individuals to adapt to changing circumstances, bounce back from setbacks, and stay committed to their vision of a brighter future.

Maintaining a **positive inner dialogue** is instrumental in goal pursuit. Self-doubt and self-criticism can be remnants of past narcissistic relationships, but practicing self-compassion and self-affirmation can counteract these negative thought patterns.

Sharing goals and aspirations with a **support system** of friends, family, or a therapist can provide encouragement and accountability. These trusted individuals can offer guidance, celebrate achievements, and provide perspective during challenging times.

Envisioning a brighter future involves **visualizing the desired outcome**. Visualization techniques can help individuals stay motivated and maintain focus on their goals. It's like creating a mental roadmap that guides them toward their vision.

Flexibility is key in goal setting. Life is full of unexpected twists, and individuals must be willing to **adapt their goals when necessary**. This adaptability ensures that pursuing a brighter future remains resilient in the face of change.

Recognizing and **celebrating achievements**, no matter how small, is crucial for maintaining motivation. Each step forward is a testament to personal growth and progress, and acknowledging these milestones reinforces a sense of accomplishment.

Setting goals and envisioning a brighter future is not just about achieving specific outcomes; it's about reclaiming agency over one's life. It's a declaration of self-worth, resilience, and determination to create a life that aligns with personal values and aspirations. In the aftermath of a narcissistic relationship, this process becomes a powerful tool for healing, growth, and embracing a future filled with hope and possibility.

In our example for Bella, Bella can work through her goals as part of her journey to rebuild her life after Jack and envision a brighter future by following these three tips:

1. **Start Small and Build Confidence:** Bella can begin by setting achievable, smaller goals that align with her larger aspirations. This approach allows her to build confidence and momentum. For example, if her long-term goal is to pursue a new career path, she can start by researching educational

programs or updating her resume. Achieving these initial milestones will boost her self-esteem and motivate her to tackle more significant objectives.

2. **Prioritize Self-Care:** Bella should prioritize self-care as she works towards her goals. Self-care encompasses physical, emotional, and mental well-being. She must manage stress, practice self-compassion, and maintain a healthy work-life balance. When Bella takes care of her overall well-being, she's better equipped to stay focused, resilient, and motivated as she pursues her goals.

3. **Seek Support and Accountability:** Bella can benefit from seeking support and accountability from her support system. Whether it's friends, family members, or a therapist, sharing her goals and progress with others provides encouragement and motivation. These individuals can offer guidance, celebrate her achievements, and give a sense of accountability, helping her stay on track with her aspirations.

By starting small, prioritizing self-care, and seeking support, Bella can effectively work through her goals and pave the way for a brighter and more fulfilling future, even in the aftermath of a challenging narcissistic relationship.

Rebuilding social connections and fostering healthy relationships

Rebuilding social connections and fostering healthy relationships is crucial to healing and starting over, especially after the challenges of a narcissistic relationship. This process provides emotional support and plays a pivotal role in reintegrating individuals into a supportive community where they can thrive.

Rebuilding social connections begins with ***self-acceptance and the establishment of healthy boundaries***. Individuals must first accept and embrace themselves, recognizing their worth and value outside the context of the narcissistic relationship. Setting and enforcing boundaries is essential to protect their emotional well-being and ensure that new relationships are respectful and nurturing.

One of the initial steps in rebuilding social connections is ***reconnecting with friends and family*** who may have been pushed away during the narcissistic relationship. These existing relationships can provide a strong support system and a sense of belonging. Rebuilding these connections requires open communication, vulnerability, and a willingness to address any strains that may have developed.

Individuals can benefit from ***expanding their social circles beyond existing connections***. Engaging in social activities, joining clubs or groups aligned with personal interests, or volunteering in the community can provide opportunities to meet like-minded individuals. These shared interests create a foundation for meaningful connections and friendships.

Building healthy relationships involves **_trust and vulnerability_**. Individuals who have experienced narcissistic abuse may struggle with trust issues. It's essential to remember that not everyone is the same as the narcissistic partner. As trust is gradually rebuilt, individuals can practice healthy vulnerability by sharing their experiences and emotions with trusted friends or potential new friends.

In some cases, individuals may benefit from **_seeking professional support_**, such as therapy or counseling, to navigate the complexities of rebuilding social connections. Therapists can offer guidance on building healthy relationships, addressing trust issues, and recognizing potential red flags in new relationships.

Rebuilding social connections should involve the **_recognition of red flags_** that may indicate unhealthy relationships. Maintaining healthy boundaries and not tolerating behaviors reminiscent of a narcissistic relationship is crucial. Individuals should trust their instincts and prioritize their well-being when assessing new connections.

Fostering healthy relationships also requires **_effective communication skills_**. Individuals can improve their ability to express their needs, listen actively, and resolve conflicts constructively. Strong communication forms the basis for respectful and fulfilling connections.

Healthy relationships involve reciprocity—both **_giving and receiving support_**. Individuals should be willing to offer help and be receptive to assistance when needed. This support strengthens connections and fosters a sense of mutual care.

Rebuilding social connections takes time, and it's essential to be ***patient with oneself***. Individuals should practice self-compassion, recognizing that setbacks are part of the journey. Self-forgiveness is crucial when navigating the complexities of forming new relationships.

Rebuilding social connections and fostering healthy relationships is vital to healing and starting over after a narcissistic relationship. By prioritizing these aspects, individuals can create a network of supportive, nurturing relationships that contribute to their well-being and personal growth.

Bella worries that she won't be able to form healthy relationships in the future. Some of the proactive steps Bella can take to ensure that she forms healthy relationships in the future, building on her journey of healing and self-discovery, are:

1. **Self-Awareness and Boundaries:** Bella should continue cultivating self-awareness and maintaining healthy boundaries. By understanding her own values, needs, and triggers, she can communicate them effectively to potential partners. Healthy boundaries are essential in any relationship, as they establish mutual respect and ensure Bella's well-being remains a priority.

2. **Red Flags Recognition:** Bella should be vigilant in recognizing red flags in potential relationships. Having experienced a narcissistic relationship, she may be more attuned to certain behaviors that signal unhealthy dynamics. It's crucial for her to trust her instincts and not ignore warning signs. She can seek guidance from trusted friends or a therapist if unsure about a potential partner's behavior.

3. **Seek Support and Therapy:** Bella can continue to seek support through therapy or counseling to navigate her journey toward forming healthy relationships. A therapist can help her process past trauma, work on self-esteem and trust issues, and develop strategies for building and maintaining fulfilling relationships. Professional guidance provides valuable tools for recognizing and addressing any lingering effects of the narcissistic relationship.

By prioritizing self-awareness, healthy boundaries, red flag recognition, and ongoing therapy, Bella can take proactive steps to ensure that she forms and maintains healthy relationships in the future. These strategies empower her to build connections built on respect, mutual support, and genuine emotional intimacy.

Exploring new hobbies and interests

Exploring new hobbies and interests is a transformative journey that can be pivotal in healing, personal growth, and starting over after a challenging experience like a narcissistic relationship. Here's an exploration of the significance and benefits of pursuing new hobbies and interests:

After a narcissistic relationship, individuals often find that their passions and interests may have been suppressed or overshadowed. Engaging in new hobbies allows them to **rediscover the joy and excitement of pursuing activities** they are genuinely passionate about. It's an opportunity to reconnect with their authentic selves and the things that bring them happiness.

Exploring new hobbies and interests allows one to **expand one's horizons**. It encourages individuals to step outside their comfort zones and try activities they may have never considered. This expansion of experiences can lead to personal growth and a broader perspective on life.

Success in learning and mastering a new hobby can significantly **boost self-esteem**. It provides a sense of accomplishment and reinforces the idea that individuals can grow and achieve. These small victories contribute to rebuilding self-confidence, which may have been eroded during a narcissistic relationship.

Engaging in hobbies is a **healthy outlet for processing emotions**. Whether through creative pursuits like art, music, or writing or physical activities like hiking or dancing, hobbies offer a constructive way to express and manage feelings. This can be particularly therapeutic for those dealing with the aftermath of emotional trauma.

Many hobbies and interests naturally **reduce stress and promote relaxation**. Activities such as meditation, gardening, or practicing a musical instrument can have a calming effect, helping individuals manage the anxiety or tension that often accompanies the recovery process.

Pursuing new hobbies can also lead to **opportunities for social connection**. Joining clubs, classes, or groups related to one's interests allows individuals to meet like-minded people and build supportive social networks. These connections can be instrumental in combatting feelings of isolation.

Engaging in hobbies provides designated *time for self-care*. It encourages individuals to prioritize their well-being and allocate time for enjoyable activities. This self-nurturing aspect of hobbies is essential in the healing and recovery process.

Exploring new hobbies can introduce a *sense of purpose and direction*. It gives individuals goals to work towards and something to look forward to. Having a purpose can be a powerful motivator in moving forward and building a fulfilling life.

Trying new hobbies involves facing challenges and learning from failures. This process contributes to *resilience building* as individuals develop the ability to bounce back from setbacks and persevere in the face of obstacles.

Pursuing new hobbies is an act of *reclaiming independence and autonomy*. It allows individuals to focus on their personal growth and interests, free from the constraints or control of a narcissistic partner.

Exploring new hobbies and interests is a multi-faceted journey that offers numerous benefits for healing and starting over. It promotes self-discovery, emotional well-being, and personal growth. It provides a path toward joy, fulfillment, and a renewed sense of purpose, allowing individuals to move forward with optimism and resilience after the challenges of a narcissistic relationship.

It doesn't have to be a new hobby that you embark on. Bella loved to paint, but Jack's relentless criticism shattered her confidence. Rediscovering her passion for painting can be a transformative experience for Bella, allowing her to heal and regain her self-confidence. Here are three tips to help her reignite her love for painting:

1. **Start Privately:** Bella can begin her artistic journey in a safe and private space. Instead of immediately sharing her work with others, she can create art solely for herself. This allows her to reconnect with the joy of painting without fearing criticism. Bella can experiment with different techniques, colors, and subjects, focusing on self-expression rather than external validation.

2. **Seek Positive Feedback:** Bella should seek out a supportive and nurturing community of fellow artists or art enthusiasts. Joining art classes, workshops, or online forums where constructive feedback and encouragement are prioritized can boost her confidence. Positive interactions with others who appreciate her art can counteract the negative impact of Jack's criticism and remind her of her artistic talents.

3. **Set Small Goals:** To rebuild her confidence gradually, Bella can set achievable and incremental goals for her painting practice. Starting with small projects or challenges allows her to track her progress and celebrate each accomplishment. As she gains confidence, she can take on more ambitious projects and explore her artistic potential further.

By starting privately, seeking positive feedback from a supportive community, and setting small goals, Bella can rediscover her passion for painting and reclaim her creative identity, free from the shackles of Jack's criticism. This process empowers her to heal and rebuild her self-esteem through the transformative power of art.

Embracing Personal Growth and Self-Empowerment

Embracing personal growth and self-empowerment is a pivotal aspect of the journey to healing and starting over, particularly after the challenges of a narcissistic relationship. This profound and transformative process empowers individuals to take control of their lives, cultivate resilience, and reach their fullest potential. Here is a comprehensive exploration of the importance and benefits of embracing personal growth and self-empowerment:

Personal growth begins with ***self-discovery and self-awareness***. Individuals who have experienced a narcissistic relationship may have lost touch with their true selves. Embracing personal growth involves introspection, reflection, and a deep understanding of one's values, strengths, weaknesses, and aspirations. This self-awareness serves as a foundation for personal development.

Many survivors of narcissistic abuse carry emotional scars from their past experiences. Embracing personal growth means ***addressing and healing past wounds***. It involves seeking therapy or counseling to process trauma, confront negative thought patterns, and develop coping strategies. This process is essential for breaking free from the emotional chains of the past.

Personal growth fosters resilience—the ability to bounce back from adversity. Survivors of narcissistic relationships have endured manipulation and emotional turmoil, making resilience a valuable asset. Through personal growth, individuals learn to navigate challenges, setbacks, and uncertainty with grace and strength. This resilience enables them to overcome obstacles and thrive.

Self-empowerment empowers individuals to **set and pursue meaningful goals**. It involves crafting a vision for the future and developing a clear path to achieve it. Whether the goals are related to career, education, personal relationships, or self-improvement, personal growth equips individuals with the determination and motivation to make their dreams a reality.

Embracing personal growth **bolsters confidence and self-esteem**. Survivors of narcissistic abuse often struggle with self-doubt and a diminished sense of self-worth. Through self-empowerment, individuals recognize their inherent value and strengths. They gain the confidence to assert themselves, make decisions, and stand up for their needs and boundaries.

Personal growth is crucial in *fostering healthy relationships*. It empowers individuals to recognize and seek out relationships based on mutual respect, trust, and emotional support. They create the foundation for fulfilling and nurturing connections by valuing themselves and setting healthy boundaries.

Personal growth encourages individuals to **embrace change** as an opportunity for growth rather than a source of fear. It involves stepping out of comfort zones, taking calculated risks, and adapting to new circumstances. Survivors of narcissistic relationships can harness their resilience to thrive in the face of change and uncertainty.

Personal growth often involves **acquiring knowledge and skills that empower individuals** to take charge of their lives. This may include pursuing education, learning new practical skills, or expanding one's emotional intelligence. Knowledge equips individuals with the tools to make informed decisions and achieve their goals.

Connecting with a supportive community often facilitates personal growth. Surrounding oneself with like-minded individuals, mentors, or therapists who encourage personal development can be invaluable. These connections provide guidance, accountability, and a sense of belonging on the journey of growth.

Ultimately, personal growth empowers individuals to ***live authentically*** and in alignment with their true selves. It means shedding the expectations and judgments of others and embracing one's uniqueness. This authentic living is a testament to inner strength and self-empowerment.

Embracing personal growth and self-empowerment is a profound journey that offers numerous benefits for survivors of narcissistic relationships. This process empowers individuals to take control of their lives, overcome past trauma, and ultimately thrive in a world of limitless possibilities.

For Bella, taking these steps toward personal growth and self-empowerment facilitates her healing and transformation and positions her to be the best mother she can be for Sofia. By focusing on her own well-being and personal development, Bella sets a powerful example of resilience and self-care for her daughter. This positive transformation allows Bella to provide Sofia with the love, stability, and support she needs to thrive.

Bella's commitment to personal growth equips her with the tools to break free from the lingering effects of her past relationship with Jack, ensuring that her daughter is shielded from any negative impact. By fostering resilience and self-confidence, Bella creates a nurturing environment where Sofia can feel safe and valued.

Furthermore, as Bella sets and pursues her own goals, she demonstrates the importance of ambition, determination, and self-belief to Sofia. This valuable life lesson encourages Sofia to dream big and work toward her own aspirations.

Bella's newfound ability to cultivate healthy relationships becomes a blueprint for Sofia's future understanding of healthy connections. By modeling strong boundaries, self-respect, and mutual respect, Bella instills the foundations of healthy interpersonal dynamics in Sofia.

Ultimately, Bella's journey of personal growth is a gift to Sofia—a gift of empowerment, love, and the promise of a brighter future. Through her transformation, Bella becomes the best version of herself and the best mother she can be, ensuring that Sofia grows up in an environment filled with positivity, support, and the potential for boundless achievements.

Conclusion

In the tumultuous journey of divorcing a narcissist, you have traveled through seven vital chapters, each laden with lessons and insights that empower us to emerge stronger, wiser, and more resilient. Your voyage began with a deep dive into the complex realm of narcissism in **Understanding Narcissism**. Armed with knowledge, you ventured further into the heart of these challenging relationships in **Recognizing Narcissistic Relationships**, where you learned to distinguish between the genuine and the deceptive.

The pivotal moment arrived in **Making the Decision to Leave**. With courage as your guide, you embarked on the path to freedom, vowing not to be trapped by manipulation and abuse any longer. **Navigating the Legal Process** gave you the tools to protect your rights and lay the foundation for a better future.

Co-parenting with a narcissist illuminated the challenging road ahead for those with children, offering strategies to safeguard the well-being of the most precious part of your life. In **Recovery and Healing**, you explored the profound transformation that personal growth and self-empowerment can bring. These chapters paved the way for **Starting Over: Building a New Life**, where you rediscovered your identity, set goals, rebuilt social connections, and embraced the path to healing.

The importance of continued self-care and growth remained a guiding principle throughout this journey. Nurturing our well-being is not a luxury but a necessity. And as you stand on the precipice of a new beginning, take this wisdom with you, and forge ahead with resilience and optimism.

As this journey concludes, be encouraged and full of hope for a fulfilling life post-divorce. Remember that your past does not define you, and your worth is immeasurable. Your challenges have sculpted you into a stronger, more empathetic, and more resilient individual. With continued self-care and growth, you will craft a future filled with happiness, fulfillment, and love.

May your life be a testament to the power of resilience, the beauty of self-discovery, and the boundless potential that lies within you. Embrace each day as a new opportunity, for the best is yet to come.

The Last Bit

Dear me,

In the midst of healing, remember to be kind to yourself. You've endured hardships that have tested your strength, but you're still here, and that's an incredible feat. It takes time to rebuild, to rediscover your identity, and to nurture the wounds inflicted by the past. Be patient with yourself; there's no need to rush. You are on a path to recovery, and you'll get there.

There will be moments when progress seems slow, and that's okay. Each step you take, no matter how small, is a step forward. Trust in your resilience and the power of personal growth. Embrace self-compassion as you would offer it to a dear friend. You are deserving of love, care, and happiness.

Remember, you are not alone on this journey. Reach out for support, connect with those who uplift and understand you, and seek professional guidance if needed. Together, we'll navigate the path to healing, rediscovering your identity, and embracing a brighter future.

You are stronger than you know, and you are going to be okay. Believe in yourself, for your potential is boundless.

With kindness, resilience and love,

Your future self xx

About the Author

Emily R. Sterling is an author dedicated to helping individuals navigate the challenging terrain of divorce with resilience and hope. Emily's background is a unique blend of psychology, personal development, and law, making her a well-rounded expert in understanding the complexities of toxic relationships and legal complexities surrounding divorce.

You won't find Emily if you go searching for her. Emily is a pen name. Rest assured though, with qualifications in law, study in psychology, and a lot of life experience, Emily possesses a profound understanding of human behavior, the legal intricacies of divorce proceedings, and the emotional toll that difficult relationships can take on individuals. Emily's extensive knowledge of family law provides readers with invaluable insights into protecting their rights and well-being during a divorce.

Emily's writing draws from her personal experiences and professional expertise to offer practical guidance and emotional support. Her compassionate approach empowers readers to break free from toxic relationships, set healthy boundaries, and rebuild their lives with resilience and hope. Emily believes everyone deserves a chance at a brighter future and is committed to helping individuals heal, grow, and thrive after divorce.

Beyond her writing, Emily is an advocate for mental health awareness and empowerment. She is deeply committed to supporting individuals as they embark on their journey to recovery and personal growth.

Emily's words serve as a guiding light for those seeking solace and strength in the face of adversity, reminding them that they can emerge from narcissistic divorce stronger and more resilient than ever.

Printed in Great Britain
by Amazon